D1546518

C. S. Lewis
on the Fullness of Life

C. S. Lewis
on the Fullness of Life

**Longing for
Deep Heaven**

DENNIS J. BILLY, CSsR

PAULIST PRESS
New York • Mahwah, NJ

The scripture quotations contained herein are from the New Revised Standard Version: Catholic Edition Copyright© 1989 and 1993 by the Division of Christian Education of the National Council of the Churches of Christ in the United States of America. Used by permission. All Rights Reserved.

Cover design by Sharyn Banks
Book design by John Eagleson

Copyright © 2009 by Dennis J. Billy, C.Ss.R.

All rights reserved. No part of this book may be reproduced or transmitted in any form or by any means, electronic or mechanical, including photocopying, recording, or by any information storage and retrieval system without permission in writing from the Publisher.

Library of Congress Cataloging-in-Publication Data

Billy, Dennis Joseph.
    C.S. Lewis on the fullness of life : longing for deep heaven / Dennis J. Billy.
       p. cm.
    Includes bibliographical references (p.).
    ISBN 978-0-8091-4543-0 (alk. paper)
    1. Jesus Christ – Person and offices. 2. Heaven – Christianity. 3. Lewis, C. S. (Clive Staples), 1898–1963. I. Title.
    BT203.B535 2009
    230 – dc22

                                 2008025814

Published by Paulist Press
997 Macarthur Boulevard
Mahwah, New Jersey 07430

www.paulistpress.com

Printed and bound in the
United States of America

In loving memory of
Itria Marino
"Aunt Lilly"
(1906–2004)

Joy is the serious business of heaven.

—C. S. Lewis

Contents

Acknowledgments

Earlier versions of material in this book have appeared elsewhere under the following titles: "The Cross in God: A Lenten Meditation," *The Priest* 61, no. 2 (2005): 37–39 [chapter 2]; *Into Your Hands: A Meditation on Jesus' Seven Last Words* (Louisville, KY: Wasteland Press, 2004), 2–4, 9–10, 50, 62, 72, 76, 90–91, 95–96 [chapter 2]; "Reaching the Alienated Heart: An Interpretation of Jesus' Descent into Hell," *Review for Religious* 64 (2005): 118–28 [chapter 3]; "Proclaiming the Easter Message: The Relevance of the Resurrection," *The Priest* 57, no. 4 (2001): 13–20, reprinted in *There Is a Season: Living the Liturgical Year* (Liguori, MO: Liguori Publications, 2001), 73–90 [chapter 4]; "Towards Deep Heaven: The Last Judgment and Catholic Imagination," *Review for Religious* 63 (2004): 342–51 [chapter 6].

Introduction

Hell is a state of mind.... And every state of mind, left to itself, every shutting up of the creature within the dungeon of its own mind — is, in the end, hell. But heaven is not a state of mind. Heaven is reality itself. All that is fully real is heavenly. For all that can be shaken will be shaken and only the unshakable remains.　　— C. S. Lewis, *The Great Divorce*

HAVE YOU EVER HEARD of Deep Heaven? Do you know where it is? Would you like to go there? Do you know how to get there? Deep Heaven is the image of humanity's celestial home in C. S. Lewis's popular Christian fantasy *The Great Divorce*.[1] It is the place where human beings must go if they wish to enjoy the fullness of life. It lies on the other side of death and requires a long and arduous journey to get there, one involving a great deal of persistence and steadfast determination.

Written over sixty years ago, Lewis's highly imaginative fantasy of life in the hereafter describes in fine detail a chartered bus ride from hell to heaven. The travelers on this bus are free to make this trip at regular intervals from a dismal gray town deep in the underworld. Those making the excursion come out of a small crack in a rock and suddenly find themselves in a much larger world just on the outskirts of heaven. Finding themselves in a place where they are less real than the world around them, they feel like phantoms and find it hard to walk on the grass and gravel pathways of this deeper (and more real) arrangement of time and space. When they look around and talk to those who have been sent to meet them, they come to different conclusions about how to proceed.

Some decide to make an even more arduous journey to God, who lives far away beyond distant mountains. Others decide to return to hell because they find it too painful to continue. Others never even get on the bus in the first place. Instead they decide to isolate themselves from human contact by wandering further and further into the lonely reaches of hell. Before long, they are great distances from the bus stop that offers them a glimpse of this other world. Eventually, even the knowledge of the existence of the bus stop for heaven is lost to their memory. A dialogue between one of the passengers who took the trip and a guide sent to meet him at the outskirts of heaven goes like this:

> "But I don't understand. Is judgment not final? Is there really a way out of Hell into Heaven?"
>
> "It depends on the way ye're using the words. If they leave that grey town behind it will not have been Hell. To any that leaves it, it is Purgatory. And perhaps ye had better not call this country Heaven. Not *Deep Heaven*, ye understand." (Here he smiled at me.) "Ye can call it the Valley of the Shadow of Life. And yet to those who stay here it will have been Heaven from the first. And ye can call those sad streets in the town yonder the Valley of the Shadow

of Death: but to those who remain there they will have been in Hell even from the beginning."[2]

Lewis achieves through narrative what the church has forgotten how to do through its doctrinal formulations — capture the Christian imagination! He does so by writing a story that collapses eternity into the space-time continuum and develops the various thought processes that lead the characters in the story to decide things the way they do. Central to his presentation is the mysterious interplay between human freedom and divine grace. Those who make the journey to Deep Heaven can do so only with help from above. Those who do not make it simply refuse this help and decide to go their own way. When viewed in this light, final judgment is more a matter of personal choice than of divine rejection. People are permitted to judge for themselves, to make their own decisions about things of ultimate value. God allows us to choose our own destiny. The doctrine of final judgment reminds us of the power of human choice and its capacity to reject even passionate and loving overtures of the living God.

As Christians we believe that Jesus of Nazareth is the person who opened up the terrain of Deep Heaven to human occupancy and blazed a trail there for others to follow. He did so through his death on the cross and rising to new life on Easter morning. We make our way to Deep Heaven not by mimicking Jesus' life and focusing on a mere external imitation of his actions, but by entering into communion with him so that our whole lives may be transformed from the inside out. The way to Deep Heaven lies in fostering an intimate friendship with Jesus. We do so by spending time with him, by listening to him, and by talking to him. The plain truth of the matter is that the closer we get to Jesus the more will we be like him. His actions will become our actions and our actions his. Our lives will no longer be our own, for Christ will truly be living in us — and we in him.

This book reflects this basic spiritual truth. Using Lewis's metaphor of Deep Heaven and helped by insights from some of his other works, we will look at six important aspects of our faith in Jesus and examine their relevance for us as we undergo this process of transformation and make our way to our celestial home. Chapter 1, "Divining the Human," looks at the mystery of the incarnation and finds there the basis of the call to enter the worlds of others to become one with them. Chapter 2, "Giving One's Life," focuses on Jesus' offering on the cross and finds there a response to human suffering that we too are called to embrace. Chapter 3, "Reaching the Alienated," examines Jesus' descent into hell in the light of our call as his followers to reach out to the despondent and marginalized. Chapter 4, "Overcoming Death," points to Christ's resurrection as evidence of a life in which we too are called to share. Chapter 5, "Returning Home," shows how Jesus' ascension into heaven completes his selfless outpouring on our behalf and points out its repercussions for our spiritual lives. Chapter 6, "Longing for Deep Heaven," finds in what we as Christians believe about the afterlife a call to put aside false gods and pray with Jesus for the coming of the kingdom.

Taken together, these chapters tell us that our desire for Deep Heaven has every bit as much to do with exploring the deepest yearnings of our hearts as it does with penetrating the unfathomable mysteries of divine love. Deep Heaven, in other words, is not a place, but an even deeper reality that first grounds us and then orients us to the true north of our existence. Its most prominent feature is what the Christian tradition calls "beatitude," which some prefer to call "happiness" or, better yet, "joy." C. S. Lewis describes joy as "an unsatisfied desire which is itself more desirable than any other satisfaction."[3] Ronald Rolheiser calls it "delight," the polar opposite of "depression" and something aligned very closely to what he refers to as "the holy longing."[4] In the context of Deep Heaven, it represents *a continual yearning for God that flows, at one and the same time, both from and toward an ever-deepening friendship with Christ.*

One of the little-known truths of the Christian faith is that those of us who long for Deep Heaven never actually find it but are instead found by it. Jesus brings it with him as part and parcel of the friendship he forges with us. A wise contemplative once put it this way: "Our discovery of God is, in a way, God's discovery of us. We cannot go to heaven to find Him because we have no way of knowing where heaven is or what it is. He comes down from heaven and finds us."[5] Deep Heaven lies in the very heart of God. We go there by allowing God to come to us and work his transforming wonders within us. It is the result of the mutual indwelling of souls that comes when two persons become close, intimate friends. Because of our friendship with Christ, heaven is unique for each of us: "Your place in heaven will seem to be made for you and you alone, because you were made for it — made for it stitch by stitch as a glove is made for a hand."[6]

St. Alphonsus de Liguori said that "paradise for God is the human heart."[7] If this is so, then Deep Heaven lies within both God's heart and our own. One thing that stands out about close friends is the way they mold each other over time and come to resemble one another with similar tastes, opinions, and ways of acting. Because they spend so much time in each other's company, they begin to anticipate each other's thoughts and actions and take them into consideration when making their own decisions. The whole point of this book is that the deeper we enter into friendship with Jesus the more will he and what we believe about him influence our lives and lead us to experience the joy of Deep Heaven.

It has been said that "an unexamined life is not worth living."[8] To help readers rise to the occasion and meet this challenge, each chapter ends with a series of reflection questions to help uncover some of the practical implications of this book for one's life. These, in turn, are followed by another section, entitled "Praying for Deep Heaven," which contains a series of meditative prayers drawing specific connections between the particular belief under consideration and our relationship with God. These questions and prayers have been included for those wishing to reflect on and ponder the material in a different light. They are included solely as aids for spiritual reflection and seek to remind the reader of the difference between *merely knowing about something* and *doing something about it.*

As St. Augustine remarks: "It is one thing to see the land of peace from a wooded ridge...and another to tread the road that leads to it."[9]

Chapter One

Divining the Human

Here and here only in all time the myth must have become fact; the Word, flesh; God, Man. This is not "a religion," nor "a philosophy." It is the summing up and actuality of them all.
— C. S. Lewis, *Surprised by Joy*

THERE WAS A TIME in my life when I had a difficult time believing in the incarnation. It seemed ludicrous to entertain the idea that God would enter history by becoming a man and walking the earth. I believed that humanity had become enlightened and long past the need for myths. The incarnation, to my mind, was nothing other than part of an adaptation of the old pagan myth of the dying and rising god, whose annual cyclical movement from death to new life marked the change of seasons and the passing of years. Even though I was raised to believe that God was born of the Virgin Mary and given the name Jesus, I connected this in my mind with just another make-believe story that, along with Santa Claus and the Easter Bunny, I had to shed as I left childhood and grew to maturity.

As the years passed, I discovered that I could not have been more wrong. What changed me was an encounter with some deeply committed and very well-educated Christians who were able to listen to my doubts and uncertainties and help me turn around midstream and navigate my way back to the headwaters of the Christian faith.

C. S. Lewis once said that "the heart of Christianity is a myth which is also a fact."[1] The incarnation, in his mind, transcends myth, but does not cease being myth. It is myth that has entered the historical confines of time and space: "If ever a myth had become fact, had become incarnated, it would be just like this."[2] For Lewis, the myths of old were nothing but faint reflections of a deeper reality still to come, a foreshadowing of events that would begin to unfold in Bethlehem of Judea during the reign of the Roman emperor Caesar Augustus.

I gradually came to see that the problem was not the incarnation but my own assumption about what was (and was not) possible. If God existed and was all-powerful, why couldn't he enter our world and become one of us? Why couldn't he be born of a virgin and enter this world as a defenseless child? Why couldn't he do something that would shatter our smug assumptions and surprise us with a new way of thinking about the relationship between the human and divine? I gradually came to see that I had very much to learn about Jesus Christ and the religion that bears his name.

A Radical Belief

If we wish to make our way to Deep Heaven, we must first understand that God entered our world and became one of us. The mystery of the incarnation is a radical belief, for it tells us that God became human and gave himself to us completely in order to reveal the fullness of the Father's love. Belief in God's enduring love for humanity lies at the very heart of the Christian message and should be central to our spiritual lives. The scene of Mary and Joseph with their newborn child in the stable at Bethlehem reminds us of the depths of God's love and the great lengths that he went to show it.

What does the mystery of the incarnation mean today? We may say the words often enough — "He was conceived by the power of the Holy Spirit and born of the Virgin Mary"[3] — but what do we understand by them? Why do we utter them? Do we truly believe them? Are they critical to our faith? The incarnation affirms that God did not merely create the world, but also entered it as one of us, becoming human at a specific point in time so that we might become sharers in the divine nature. This belief in Emmanuel, a name meaning "God is with us" (see Mt 1:23), is a unique characteristic of Christianity and sets it apart from the other major world religions.

The word "incarnation," from the Latin word meaning "to be made flesh," refers to the mystery of the Word of God becoming a man some two thousand years ago in the person of Jesus of Nazareth. It took centuries for the church to understand the relationship between the divine and human in Jesus. Its official teaching, moreover, does not preclude still deeper insights in the future. As understood today, the teaching affirms that Jesus of Nazareth was both God and man, an individual who was, at one and the same time, both fully human and fully divine. The Word of God assumed our humanity and exists in an intimate union with it as one divine person. Jesus of

Nazareth, in other words, was not just a man of God, but God himself. God's only Son was conceived in a woman's womb and born into this world as one of us. This "Grand Miracle," as Lewis calls it, would change the course of human history and, even more importantly, bring new life to the human heart.[4]

The main reason for the incarnation is so God could give us a share in his divine life. Behind this idea lies the assumption that we are incapable of reaching God on our own, so God must come to us. God himself bridges the infinite distance between the divine and the human so that we may receive the benefits of intimate fellowship with the divine.

In the words of St. Athanasius (295–373): "God became human so that humanity might become divine."[5] By becoming one of us, God made it possible for us to participate in his divine life. We share in this life in, with, and through the Word who, as the eternal and only-begotten Son of the Father, extends to us the benefits of adopted sonship and enables us to live as children of God. Because of Jesus, God has adopted us as his children and makes no distinction between his love for his Son and his love for us.

God entered our world, however, not only to help us, but also to show us what it means to be human. "The glory of God," St. Irenaeus (c. 130–c. 200) tells us, "is a living human person." The latter part of this phrase is often translated as "a human person fully alive."[6] God became human in Jesus Christ to reveal to us the depths of our humanity. Jesus gives glory to the Father by demonstrating to us what it means to be fully alive, that is, completely in touch with and at home in our humanity.

Those who believe in his message and follow him seek to befriend their humanity and make it an integral part of their relationship to the Father. They do so by placing their trust in the risen Lord so that his glorified humanity might reinvigorate their own and they might partake in the first fruits of the new creation.

Paradise for God

How does this come about? To share in this new creation we must become once more like little children. Jesus himself reminds us of this necessity: "Truly I tell you, whoever does not receive the kingdom of God as a little child will never enter it" (Mk 10:15). Just as an infant child is helpless and dependent on its parents for everything, so too must we look to God and depend on him for all our needs. We become like little children through baptism, when we are immersed in the renewing water of Christ's paschal mystery and become members of his body. Because of our special relationship with Jesus made possible by this sacrament, God now looks upon us as his adopted children. As a result, we too can turn to him as a loving parent and cry out to him, "Abba, Father" (Mk 14:36).

Jesus must have known very well what it meant to be like a little child. He relied on God, his Father, for all things. He also saw in his mother, Mary, the model woman of faith and the mother of all believers (see Jn 19:26). Hans Urs von Balthasar speaks of Jesus in this way: "God's eternal Word was once a child — and hence he has always remained a child. He became a child of men because he was never, nor ever will be, anything other than the eternal child of the Father. Because he was once the child of men, he can constantly reveal his eternal childlikeness in a form that is human and intelligible to humans."[7] These words remind us that God also became human to enable us to contemplate the face of the eternal child in the infant Jesus, who, although born some two thousand years ago, is eager to be born this very day in the deepest recesses of our hearts. Sometimes when we gaze upon a newborn infant, the fragile and vulnerable Christ child within us awakes from sleep and sparks within us a deep sense of awe at the wonder and sheer mystery of life. At times like these, the mystery of the incarnation draws near to us and helps us to glimpse and better understand the great joy we celebrate at Christmas.

The application of the incarnation of the Word to our spiritual childhood goes back to the Greek fathers and is also present in some Latin theologians. The medieval Dominican friar Meister Eckhardt (c. 1260–1327/28), for example, speaks of the Word eternally begotten by the Father, born of the Virgin Mary, and birthed spiritually in our hearts through the power of the Holy Spirit.[8] This powerful metaphor highlights the basic continuity in the Christian beliefs in the Trinity, incarnation, and our sanctification. What is especially significant for our present purposes is the way it provides a broader context for our understanding the meaning of God's becoming human. The doctrine of the incarnation, in other words, would make little sense if the Eternal Word was not being eternally generated by the Father or if the process of the Word's becoming flesh would not have strong repercussions for the conversion and spiritual renewal of our hearts. "The paradise of God," St. Alphonsus de Liguori (1696–1787) tells us, "is the human heart."[9] The ultimate goal of the incarnation is for God to dwell within our hearts so that we can share in his divine life. This intimate communion becomes possible through Christ's gift of self to the world and is his very reason for deciding to enter our world and become one of us.

Paradise for Us

If paradise for God is to dwell in our hearts, then paradise for us is to dwell in his. The mystery of the incarnation teaches us that true happiness lies in sharing in God's life and becoming fully alive. It also reveals a number of other important features about the nature of true happiness.

The incarnation tells us that happiness has something to do with giving ourselves to others. The Apostle Paul reminds us in his letter to the Philippians that Jesus "emptied himself, taking the form of a slave, being born in human likeness" (Phil 2:7). This giving of oneself for the sake of others lies at the very heart of the Christian message and represents the spiritual ideal that all believers strive to embody in their lives. Although God would become human only once in human history, the spiritual message behind this mystery comes from the very depths of divine love and touches our hearts in profound ways. Left to ourselves, we would never be able to love as Jesus loves. God's word is born within us spiritually, to change our hearts and enable us to open up to his love with joy and make it our own.

The incarnation tells us that happiness has something to do with allowing God's love to ground itself in our hearts. The belief that God became human so that we might become divine tells us that God can bridge the infinite chasm separating the divine and human and bring them together in us through the power of his word. The incarnation provides the means through which the eternal birth of the Word from the Father touches the human heart, dwells within it, and ultimately transforms it. It is the way God's plan for our sanctification becomes a practical reality.

The incarnation tells us that happiness involves the transformation of every aspect of our human makeup so that we can joyfully commune with God and rest in his presence. The incarnation plays a mediating role in God's saving plan for us. The union of the divine and human in Christ highlights the necessity of something from outside the bounds of our humanity to help us overcome our fragility and helplessness before God. At the same time, it tells us that God's transforming grace is not merely imputed to us from without, but heals and elevates us from within.

The incarnation tells us that happiness has something to do with our belonging to the community of believers. God's word is born not only within our hearts, but also within the church. The union of the divine and human natures in Christ is the foundation of the mystical communion of his body. Because of the incarnation, salvation is mediated to the human family first through Christ and his glorified humanity and then through the community of believers who make up his body, the church. As in the incarnation, the birth of the Word within the church takes place through a loving human embrace of the power of the Holy Spirit. Through this power, God's saving grace is poured out through Christ to the church and from there to the whole human family.

The incarnation tells us that happiness also has something to do with our relationship with Jesus' mother, Mary. God's word was born into this world through her loving and faithful fiat. Her selfless "Yes" to the angel's message grew into her joyful affirmation of the Spirit's presence in the upper room at Pentecost (see Acts 1:12–2:13). Her free and spontaneous response to God forms the basis for the deep veneration Catholics have for her. Mary is her Son's first and closest disciple. She is also the mother of the church and all believers. As such, she is also the mother of all humanity and of each human person who has ever lived. A close, intimate relationship with her will help us to foster the same with her Son.

The incarnation tells us that happiness also means living in freedom. God does not force his love upon us. For the incarnation to happen, it was necessary for someone to freely open her heart (and womb) to God in a way that would change her life for all time. Mary represents humanity's primal cooperation with the Lord's redeeming grace. To appreciate fully what happened at the precise moment of Jesus' conception, we must ponder the Virgin Mary's heart and see within it our own deepest desires and inclinations. We too desire to give birth to the word of God in our lives. What Mary accomplished by giving birth to Jesus, we accomplish in our hearts through the Spirit's grace and her constant intercession.

The incarnation tells us that happiness means living in peace with the rest of creation. Once we allow for the birth of the eternal word in the human heart, we must

recognize the significance such an event has for all creation. The Word became flesh not merely to redeem and
sanctify humanity, but to call forth a new creation. This
newness of life makes itself manifest wherever the human
heart ponders its surroundings and strives to make them
correspond to the call it perceives. The incarnation invites
us to ponder our relationship to the created world and
take responsibility for it. Such an invitation opens itself
up to dialogue with others, especially those of other religions, and their perceptions of the nature of humanity's
relationship to the rest of creation.

Finally, *the incarnation tells us* that happiness means
living in hope. The darkness in the human heart often
prevents us from recognizing our deepest longings. We
experience ourselves as being a part of both the old and
the new creations. This inner struggle already points to
Christ's presence in our midst, for we would not experience the tension if he were not in some way already with
us. Belief in Christ involves living an already-but-not-yet
existence, with our gaze fixed firmly on the present with
hope for what is yet to come.

Conclusion

The mystery of the incarnation has great relevance for our
lives. It is not a piece of fiction or an abstract dogma with
little or no practical significance, but a central doctrine of
the faith that tells us as much about ourselves as it does
about God. This foundational Christian truth is a myth
that has become a fact. It reveals the nature of God's love
for us and the way we can best reciprocate it. It highlights

the privileged place we have in God's eyes and tells us a great deal about the nature of happiness.

The mystery of the incarnation reveals God's predilection for us and our own desire for Deep Heaven. It tells us that the Word became flesh as a way of befriending us so that God might again walk in fellowship with us. For such a friendship to develop, however, we must first be healed of our inner wounds and raised to a divine stature. Our transformation takes place because Christ has united himself to our humanity through the ongoing gift of himself, a process that begins with the incarnation and culminates in his paschal mystery. The mystery of the incarnation proclaims the Good News of God's love for the world and the possibility of our renewed intimacy with the divine. It tells us that our way to God is intimately tied to God's way to us and that an infant child in swaddling clothes, lying in a manger in the city of David called Bethlehem some two thousand years ago, carries with him our deepest dreams and the hopes of all humanity.

Reflection Questions

1. What does the mystery of the incarnation mean to you? Do you really believe that God became a man in the person of Jesus of Nazareth? Is this belief central to your understanding of the makeup of reality? Does it contribute to your own self-understanding? Could you do without it?

2. Do you agree that God became human so that humanity might become divine? What does it mean for humanity to become divinized? How would a

divinized humanity be similar to your present experience of what it means to be human? How would it differ?

3. Do you agree with the idea of multiple births of the Eternal Word? Which of these births do you find easiest to understand? Which of them do you find most difficult to accept? Which of them do you believe in most strongly?

4. Do you believe that paradise for God is to dwell in the human heart? If so, what does such a statement say about the nature of God? If not, why not? What does it mean for God to dwell within the human heart? What does it mean for the human heart to dwell in God?

5. What significance does the incarnation have for the rest of creation? Is its purpose the transformation only of humanity or of the entire universe? What implications does it have for your relationship with other individuals and social institutions? What implications does it have for your relationship to the environment? Do any of these relationships conflict? How can the mystery of the incarnation help you to prioritize them?

Praying for Deep Heaven

I long for you, Lord, and I long for Deep Heaven.

I ponder the mystery of your incarnate Word and am overwhelmed by your great love.

You were not satisfied with merely creating me and my world.

You desired to walk in it yourself, to breathe the same air as I breathe, to feel as I feel, to sense as I sense, to suffer as I suffer, to die as I die.

You became like me so that I might become like you.

Thank you, Lord, for your eternally begotten Son, for the birth of your Word in the womb of the Virgin Mary, in the womb of your church, in the depths of my heart.

Thank you, Lord, for the eternal childhood you have revealed in the coming of your Son to the world. Thank you, Lord, and help me.

Help me to reach out to others as you have reached out to me.

Help me to enter their worlds and to stand by them as you have entered my world and stood by me.

Help me to be with them as you have been with me throughout my difficult sojourn in this life.

Help me, Lord, help me.

Help me so that I may help.

Heal me so that I might heal.

Renew me so that I might help you to make all things new, to build a new creation.

Chapter Two

Giving One's Life

He tasted death on behalf of all others. He is the representative "Die-er" of the universe: and for that very reason the Resurrection and the Life. Or conversely, because He truly lives, He truly dies, for that is the very pattern of reality. Because the higher can descend into the lower He who from all eternity has been incessantly plunging Himself in the blessed death of self-surrender to the Father can also most fully descend into the horrible and (for us) involuntary death of the body.

—C. S. Lewis, *Miracles*

AT ONE POINT in my life, one of the difficulties I had with Christianity was what I called the problem of Jesus' death. I couldn't understand why he shed his blood and gave up his life to save us. Couldn't God have found some other means to make up for our innumerable sins? It seemed cruel of God, almost barbaric, to ask his only Son to die a slow, torturous death on a Roman cross. Why would God ask such a thing? Even if Jesus died willingly, doesn't it seem strange that the Father would even consider such a drastic measure? Whenever I gazed upon Jesus' bloodied corpus, I became deeply perplexed.

I gradually came to see, however, that, try as I might, I would probably never fully understand the reasons behind Jesus' horrible death. I also began to see that it really didn't make much difference whether I understood them or not. C. S. Lewis puts it this way: "We are told that Christ was killed for us, that His death has washed out our sins, and that by dying He disabled death itself. That is the formula. That is Christianity. That is what is to be believed. Any theories we build up as to how Christ's death did all this are . . . quite secondary."[1]

Lewis helped me to see that I could accept what Christ accomplished by his death on the cross without fully understanding it. He makes a very simple point: "A man can eat his dinner without understanding exactly how food nourishes him. A man can accept what Christ has done without knowing how it works: indeed, he certainly would not know how it works until he has accepted it."[2] When it comes to Jesus' death, the basics are what really matter. Christianity tells us that Jesus' death was the supreme expression of God's love for humanity. It tells us that the blood of the cross was the way God chose to seal a New Covenant with his people and lead them to paradise. It tells us that Jesus gave up his life to lead us to Deep Heaven.

Death by Crucifixion

Hardly anyone disputes the claim that Jesus "suffered under Pontius Pilate, was crucified, died, and was buried."[3] This affirmation lies at the narrative heart of the Christian faith and provides the historical backdrop against which the events of Easter morning would unfold. Although they may differ in details, the Gospels are remarkably clear that the Romans killed the carpenter of Nazareth by direct order of the Roman procurator of Palestine. This assertion roots the Christian faith in history and gave early believers an important touchstone for their ongoing reflection on the meaning of the Christ event.

Crucifixion by the Romans took place publicly and in the open air. It began with stripping the criminal and scourging him at the place of judgment. To shame him before the people, he was then forced to carry the crossbeam of the cross naked through the streets to the place of execution. Along the way, he was mocked and often spat upon by those who lined the streets. If his strength appeared to be waning, someone was forced to carry the crossbeam for him so that he would not die before he reached the place of execution.

Once there, the naked criminal was fastened to the crossbeam by rope or by nails. He was then hoisted high in the air so that the crossbeam could rest either at the top of the vertical beam, which was permanently in place, or in a specially carved notch near the top. Above his head was placed an inscription listing the crime for which he was being executed. To augment his torments, the criminal's feet were usually fastened or nailed to a wooden support so that he would be able to breathe by pulling up from his arms and pushing down with his legs. If the legs were left dangling in the air, death would come much sooner.

When the Romans wanted to teach the people a special lesson, they raised the criminal very high in the air so that more would be able to see him. Death often took a matter of days. If the Romans were in a rush, they would hasten death by either breaking the criminal's legs or by piercing his side with a lance. The body would be left on the cross to rot. If it was close to the ground, it could even be torn apart and eaten by wild animals.

With a few notable exceptions, the accounts of Jesus' death closely resemble this routine pattern of Roman execution. The Jews had been given certain concessions by the Romans for executions taking place in Palestine. Jesus, for example, was given back his clothing after being scourged because of objections about driving a criminal naked through the streets (see Mk 15:20; Mt 27:31). In another concession to the Jews, he was offered some wine drugged with myrrh to numb the pain (see Mk 15:23; Mt 27:34; Jn 19:29). His body, moreover, was not left to rot on the cross but, in keeping with Jewish law (see Deut 21:23), was taken down and buried before the end of the day (see Mk 15:42–47).

Despite these few allowances, Jesus' death was horrible and excruciatingly painful. The Romans used crucifixion to break the criminal down physically, emotionally, socially, and even spiritually. In Jesus' day, it was a brutal reminder of Roman occupation and domination. Compared to crucifixion, stoning, the typical Jewish form of capital punishment, was relatively quick and painless. The Romans used fear to dominate the nations. Crucifixion was a principal tool in their repertoire, one that many feared and few had the courage to face, let alone endure. What happened to Jesus on Good Friday was exceedingly brutal but nothing unusual by Roman standards. If Pilate's order was routine and commonplace, however, Jesus' courageous embrace of death exceeded all human limits and brought the world to the threshold of the sacred.

The Cross in God

Why would Jesus embrace such horrific suffering? Did he do so freely? Was he moved by some kind of necessity? Could his death have been avoided? What does it mean for us? For centuries Christians have asked themselves these and similar questions as they reflected upon the meaning of Jesus' passion and death. Although their answers vary in details and very often reflect their surrounding historical and cultural milieus, they almost always agree that he suffered and died to free us from our sins and to manifest God's unending love for us. Christianity, however, is more than just an abstract theory about Christ's death. For C. S. Lewis, "the central Christian belief is that Christ's Death has somehow put us right with God and given us a fresh start. Theories as to how it did this are another matter. A good many different theories have been held as to how it works; what Christians all agree on is that it does work."[4] It works because Jesus' passion is not something extrinsic to God but flows from the Father's deep compassion for a broken, disheartened world.

It was once said that "there is a cross in God before the wood is seen on Calvary."[5] Some people find such words enigmatic and difficult to accept. Suffering, after all, is not a goal to strive for, but something to put up with and eventually overcome. How could suffering exist in the very heart of God? The uneasy marriage between

Greek and Hebrew thought from which early Christian
theology was forged complicates the matter further. The
Greek philosophers believed God was unchanging and
unfeeling and identified him with the three transcendental
values of the One, the True, and the Good. The Hebrew
scriptures, by way of contrast, evolved in their understanding of the divine and increasingly came up with
a loving, all-powerful, and compassionate God actively
engaged in the destiny of his people. Each of these con-
flicting understandings eventually found its way into the
orthodox Christian presentation of the doctrine of God.

Christian theologians traditionally used the Greek approach when probing the mysterious nature of God, but
followed the Hebrew point of view when reflecting upon
God's involvement in human history. By putting these two
very different understandings of divinity side by side and
insisting that both were valid representations of God's
nature, they succeeded in preserving a deep sense of the
mystery of who God was. By means of this juxtaposition,
God was recognized as the One, the True, and the Good,
but also as the God of Abraham, Isaac, and Jacob. The
church fathers believed that this very same God was
humanity's Creator, Redeemer, and Sanctifier, a Trinity
of divine persons sharing the same divine substance. They
also believed that Jesus Christ was the fullness of God's
revelation to humanity: "If you know me, you will know
my Father also. From now on you do know him and have
seen him" (Jn 14:7).

To say that there is a cross in God even before Jesus'
death on Calvary takes the Christian understanding of
God one step further and offers a profound insight into
the mystery of God's inner life. "No one has greater

love than this, to lay down one's life for one's friends"
(Jn 15:13). Jesus' crucifixion was a defining moment of
his life: it says something about who he was and what
he stood for; it should also tell us something about his
relationship to the Father.

That relationship, Christians believe, is rooted in the
intimate bond of love they share by virtue of the Spirit,
who proceeds from the Father and the Son. If God's very
nature is defined by love, then the cross, as the symbol of
love par excellence, *had* to be in God before the wood was
seen on Calvary. The difficulty comes when we recognize
that that very same cross is also a symbol of deep human
anguish.

Can love and suffering be separated? Much depends on
what we mean by the terms. There are different types of
love just as there are different types of suffering. In his
book *The Four Loves,* C. S. Lewis distinguishes divine
love from the natural loves of human friendship, romantic
love, and natural affection.[6] God's love is called "char-
ity" and is associated with the selfless giving of oneself to
another. In its human embodiment, it has been described
by Thomas Aquinas as "a certain kind of friendship with
God."[7] In its most general sense, "suffering" typically
means "enduring some kind of pain" — physical, psycho-
logical, spiritual, even social. If divine love can have a
human embodiment, perhaps human suffering or something like it can also exist in God. After all, are we not
created in God's own image and likeness? To love as
God loves does not necessarily mean that one is going to
"endure some kind of pain" for someone. It does imply,
however, that one would be willing to do so should the

need arise. That is precisely why the wood is seen on Calvary. Jesus' love is redemptive. There was a need for it.

The pain of God manifests itself in a divine self-offering: "Though he was in the form of God, did not regard equality with God as something to be exploited, but emptied himself, taking the form of a slave" (Phil 2:6–7). God does not will to suffer; he suffers because he refuses to abandon humanity to the dark powers within it.

Does God endure pain? "My Father, if this cannot pass unless I drink it, your will be done" (Mt 26:42). Who is suffering more here: the Son or the Father? Can the Father really be indifferent to the Son's pain? If so, what kind of Father would he be? Let there be no doubt, there was agony in God *before* the Son's agony in the garden and on the cross — and even *after.*

Jesus' death on the cross says something about his relationship with the Father and reveals to us something about the very nature of God. God has a heart — and it can be broken. He was willing to become one of us and die for us in order to manifest his love for us, mend our hearts, and make us whole. Our God is a God of compassion; he suffers not only *for* us, but also *with* us. The real enigma here is the way he brought together both the human and divine in the person of Jesus in order to embrace human experience and make it his own. Was there a cross in God before the wood was seen on Calvary? There certainly was. If not, Calvary would never have happened, and we would never have known the joy of God's friendship.

Through Jesus' death the cross, the symbol par excellence of Roman brutality and domination, was transformed into the distinctive symbol of a new religion. His testimony from the cross marks the beginning of this

important change. A verse from the prophet Isaiah says it
best: "They shall beat their swords into plowshares, and
their spears into pruning hooks" (Isa 2:4). Jesus teaches
us how to do so. He encountered the cross and embraced
it. He responded to the violence of the Roman Empire
with the silent message of a kingdom of another world.
Through his death, he took an instrument of death and
turned it into a lasting sign of hope and comfort for
countless millions.

The Cross in Us

Jesus' cross represents the extent to which God would go
to renew a lost and forsaken world. According to C. S.
Lewis, "The death of Christ is just that point in history at
which something absolutely unimaginable from outside
shows through into our world."[8] Through Jesus' passion
and death, God intervenes in human history in a powerful
way. Jesus dies, however, not only to change the course of
history, but also to change our hearts. His death touches
us, transforms us, and leads us to happiness and fullness
of life. It tells us that the cross of Calvary is planted not
only in God's heart, but also deep within our own. When
we ponder it, we can learn a great deal about the following of Christ, the way of discipleship that ultimately leads
us to the joy of Deep Heaven.

To begin with, Jesus' passion and death *teaches us
how to deal with failure.* Jesus' death at the hands of
the Romans was one of the most painful and humiliating of deaths imaginable. This sort of public execution
represented failure in the eyes of men and brought shame
to the individual and those connected with him. At the

time of his death, Jesus was deemed by nearly everyone a complete and utter failure. The hope he had inspired in his followers had completely dissipated; he had been left alone and literally suspended in the air to bleed profusely and eventually suffocate. In this moment of darkness, however, feeling abandoned by all, he still found the resources within himself to trust in the power of the Father's love. Jesus' death encourages us to look at our own failures and to face the shameful and humiliating moments of our lives with courage and quiet trust in God's promises.

Jesus on Calvary also *demonstrates the power of true forgiveness.* His death on the cross was an act of self-less giving. Early on in his public ministry, he taught his disciples to love their enemies and to pray for their persecutors (see Mt 5:44). As he hangs from the cross, he demonstrates that he lived what he taught — even in death. When he asks his Father to forgive his tormen-tors, he does so from a heart that within a short while would be pierced by the lance of one of the very men he is forgiving. By asking his Father to forgive, he teaches us that to hurt another person deliberately and unjustly is sin against God. The person who hurts another in this way, moreover, ultimately hurts himself or herself in the process. This self-inflicted wound is what Jesus sees when he looks down from the cross and gazes upon his tor-mentors. Moved with compassion for them, he turns to his Father in heaven and pleads with him on their behalf. He does the same for us whenever we injure ourselves in this way and bids us to do likewise with those who have injured us.

Jesus' suffering from the cross, moreover, *highlights the existential choice before each of us.* Jesus' sense of abandonment embraced every dimension of his being: the physical, the emotional, the mental, the social, and especially the spiritual. In this tortured state, he entered the depths of our broken humanity and brought it back to wholeness. He did so by confronting the powers of darkness with the power of love. His death on the cross would ultimately show that love was stronger than death and formed the underlying fabric of reality. As he hung from the cross, however, all this remained mysteriously hidden from sight. Abandoned by his Father at this critical juncture of his life, he had one fundamental choice before him: to despair of life and of all he hoped for or to trust that, even though his Father seemed so distant and far away, the Father's love would ultimately be there for him. Jesus chose the latter and never doubted his decision. Aided by his Spirit, he invites us to follow suit.

Jesus' anguished prayer from the cross *reveals to us the power of intercessory prayer.* Through his death on the cross, Jesus makes fellowship with God once again possible. He did for us something we were unable to do for ourselves. Because of our egoism and self-centeredness, it was impossible for us to rectify our relationship with God. Human nature had somehow gone awry, and only God himself could make it right again. Jesus' suffering on the cross was God's way of straightening things out. By entering our world, becoming one of us, and dying for us, God was able to intercede for us and speak to the Father on our behalf. Jesus continues to do so for us to this very day. He is our means to the Father, the path each of us must follow to pass from this life to life eternal. As his followers and members of his body, we unite our prayers to his and are able to intercede for others on their behalf.

In his death Jesus *offers us a model of true courage.* In his dying moments from the cross, Jesus was not only giving himself as an offering of self to the Father. He was also giving himself to us. His passion and death stand as a model of courage for his followers to imitate. Down through the centuries, generation upon generation of Christians would look to the cross and see in the bloodied corpus hanging from it both a challenge and a call. The challenge would be to dare to trust in him as he trusted in the Father. The call would be to pick up their own crosses and follow in his steps. Jesus' cross is always challenging and calling us. No matter where we are, it stands as a reminder of someone who gave every ounce of his life for us in order that we might live. His challenge and his call ask us to do the same for others. Jesus' death on the cross seeks to evoke from us a similar response.

Jesus' suffering *helps us to find meaning in our own suffering.* Jesus' suffering and death continue to this day in the members of his body. We who have been immersed in his paschal mystery participate in his suffering and death. We will be crucified on the crosses that we have shouldered for him and his following. We will suffer innocently from wounds inflicted upon our bodies and souls. The crucifix serves as a reminder of what Jesus went through for us and of what he is asking us to go through for him and for others. When we look at it, we are reminded that we too must face our suffering and eventual death with expectant apprehension, enduring patience, and steadfast perseverance. Our joy and zest for life will be tinged with the knowledge of a death that is to come. Our suffering in the moment will serve as a window to eternity, opening us up to the intimate life of the Godhead. Our focus on the reason and end of life will help us to face our suffering and death with steadfast perseverance. Because of Jesus' suffering and death, our own suffering and death take on new meaning. Through Christ, the power of God's love has been unleashed in the world. Jesus gives us the opportunity to share in that power and to be with him until our earthly end converges into his.

Finally, Jesus' death on Calvary *helps us to overcome our own fear of death.* "Father, into your hands I commend my spirit" (Lk 23:46). When Jesus commends his spirit to the Father, he also offers along with it the spirit of all humanity. In his final act of earthly freedom, he entrusts the human spirit — the vitality and lifeblood of the human race — to the Father's care. This act was something we could not do of our own accord. Someone had to do it for us, someone like us but also like God, someone human, but also divine. In this final act, Jesus acts as the true mediator between God and man. He takes our place before God and intercedes for us. In his last words, he prays the prayer we longed to pray, but could not. He takes us with him as he faces death and places us with him in the Father's care. We face death together, and, because we are in the Father's care, together we shall overcome it. Jesus has identified himself so closely with humanity that his story has become our story, and our story, his. Because of this close identity, we trust that he who suffered and died for us will be there for us in our time of need. Jesus identifies our needs with his needs. Anything we ask the Father in his name, we shall receive (see Jn 15:16).

Conclusion

Jesus identified with us so closely that he bore on his shoulders the full weight of our human sinfulness. His innocence replaced our guilt; his nearness to the Father, the distance separating us from the divine. Jesus entered our world not to condemn it, but to save it (see Jn 3:17). He did so by embracing death on our behalf so that our destiny could be inexorably bound up with his. His destiny was to live and die by the power of love, a force he unleashed on the world through his suffering and death on the cross.

Through the wood of the cross, Jesus defeated the power of death with the powerlessness of love. Although death had embraced Jesus by imprinting its cold, lifeless marks into his bloodied limbs and corpus, it could not subdue him, for he had overcome his fear of death and commended his spirit to his Father's care. That care would become our hope and the cause of our salvation. It would bind up our wounds and heal our hearts. It would bring us back to health and lead us to a joyful celebration of new life. It would show us the way to Deep Heaven and enable us to share with Jesus the riches of the Father's glory.

Reflection Questions

1. Why did Jesus embrace the cross so freely and willingly? Does his suffering and death tell you anything about courage in the midst of adversity? Does it tell you anything about facing one's failures?

2. Does Jesus' death on the cross tell you anything about the nature of love? What does it mean to give

oneself completely to others? Must such selfless giving always end in death? Is putting others' interests
before your own a type of dying?

3. What does Jesus' death on the cross tell you about
   the nature of spiritual abandonment? Have you
   ever experienced such abandonment? Have you ever
   experienced the depths of your broken humanity?

4. Do you believe that your own suffering is somehow
   tied up with Jesus' passion and death? If so, how
   does this belief affect your attitude toward your own
   suffering? How does it affect your attitude toward
   the suffering of others?

5. Are you afraid of death? Does the narrative of Jesus'
   suffering and death ease this fear or increase it? Do
   you believe that Jesus has overcome death? Do you
   believe his promise to do the same for you?

Praying for Deep Heaven

I long for you, Lord, and I long for Deep Heaven.

*I ponder your horrible death on the cross and am
   deeply moved by the extent of your suffering.*

*When I stop to think that you suffered and died for
   me, I am saddened all the more and moved
   to tears. Why is there so much hatred in the
   world? Why do the innocent suffer? Why do
   the just die? The answers seem to be few and
   far between.*

*Lord, you suffered and died not only to redeem us,
   but also to show us the meaning of love.*

You accepted your cross and embraced it willingly, because it was your Father's will. You faced your persecutors with courage; your death, with a heavy heart ready to break from your love for the world.

Thank you, Lord, for laying down your life for us.

Thank you for offering yourself on my behalf.

Thank you for giving yourself completely so that others might live.

Help me, Lord, help me.

Help me to accept the Father's will for me.

Help me to ponder the cross in God and to carry those he asks me to bear.

Help me to embrace with love whatever crosses come my way.

Help me to give myself to others through them.

Help me to lay down my life for my friends as we walk the way of the cross and look for the coming of your kingdom.

Chapter Three

Reaching the Alienated

There is no other doctrine which I would more willingly remove from Christianity than this [the doctrine of the final judgment], if it lay in my power. But it has the full support of Scripture and, specially, of Our Lord's own words; it has always been helped by Christendom; and it has the support of reason. If a game is played, it must be possible to lose it. If the happiness of a creature lies in self-surrender, no one can make that surrender but himself (though many can help him to make it) and he may refuse.

— C. S. Lewis, *The Problem of Pain*

I'VE ALWAYS HAD a hard time accepting the existence of Hell. It seemed inconsistent to me that a religion like Christianity could speak so eloquently about God's mercy and go on to affirm a state of existence where people were somehow beyond its pale. If God truly was all-good and all-powerful, then why couldn't he do something to make people aware of what a life of eternal separation from divine love would be like? Couldn't God touch people's hearts in such a way that they would be moved to undergo a genuine conversion? Can the human

heart really be so stubborn in resisting the gentle overtures of God's bountiful love? How could hell exist in the
midst of so much mercy?

It wasn't easy finding satisfactory answers to such questions. As far as I can tell, the only plausible reason for
hell's existence has something to do with the reality of
human freedom. God's love forces no one. He allows
people to choose their fate. Hell, as C. S. Lewis reminds
us, is where people "enjoy forever the horrible freedom
they have demanded."[1] People are there because they
want to be: "The doors of hell are locked on the *inside*."[2]
The doctrine of Jesus' descent into hell reminds us of this
somber truth.

Understanding Jesus' Descent

When we affirm Jesus' "descent into hell" or, as some
prefer to call it, his "descent among the dead," we should
make a distinction between the way it is expressed and
the truth it seeks to convey.[3] After all, there must be more
to this doctrine than the image it conjures in our minds
of a literal, spatial descent by Christ into a dark and
gloomy underworld, a notion tied more to a now outdated Hebrew worldview than the astonishing message of
God's undying love for the world. Most would agree that
hell is not so much a *place* of eternal damnation as a *state
of being* that makes one completely alienated from God.
In our understanding of hell the focus should be primarily
on the spiritual and mental rather than an overempha-
sis on the physical. When speaking about Jesus' "descent
into hell" today, perhaps it would be more appropriate
to interpret it in a way that reveals something significant

about the primal human experience of being alienated from God and about Jesus' central role in bringing that intense sense of separation to an end.

In *The Great Divorce,* C. S. Lewis describes hell as a place where people are constantly alienating themselves from one another:

> As soon as anyone arrives he settles in some street. Before he's been there twenty-four hours he quarrels with his neighbor. Before the week is over he's quarreled so badly that he decides to move. Very likely he finds the next street empty because all the people there have quarreled with *their* neighbors — and moved. So he settles in. If by any chance the street is full, he goes further. But even if he stays, it makes no odds. He's sure to have another quarrel pretty soon and then he'll move on again. Finally he'll move right out to the edge of town and build a new house.... That's how the town keeps on growing.[4]

Alienation makes us feel isolated from ourselves, one another, and God. It hinders us in our journey through life and prevents us from becoming the persons we are called to become. Ronald Rolheiser puts it this way: "We are social beings, meant to live in love and intimacy with others. Our nature demands this. When, for whatever reasons, we cannot achieve this and communicate the love as we should, then something is missing inside of us — and we feel it! We feel estranged and alienated."[5] To be in hell is to be in a state of complete and utter alienation from God. In such a state, we have lost complete touch with ourselves and, as a result, have become incapable of reaching out in love to anyone.

Most of us will admit to have experienced, at some point in our lives, this sense of being estranged from and "out of sync" with ourselves, the world around us, and the God who created us. We feel at war with ourselves, divided within yet incapable of healing that division. Although we are conscious of it in different ways and in varying degrees, this sense of alienation is not merely a matter of personal choice (although choice can contribute to it), but a part of our experience of being human. What makes matters worse is that we somehow sense that it was not meant to be this way, that something has gone terribly wrong with our human condition and that somehow humanity as a whole bears at least some (if not all) responsibility for it.

Making All Things New

Christianity is all about how God chose to make things right again by sharing our human condition and overcoming this deeply ingrained sense of alienation lurking deep in our hearts. Down through the ages, the church has developed the doctrines of original sin and redemption to explain this universal sense of alienation and reveal the way God has chosen to rectify it.

Jesus' descent into hell is intimately tied to these fundamental Christian doctrines, each of which, like two sides of a coin, cannot exist without each other. Here, too, a distinction must be made between the way these doctrines are expressed and the truths they disclose. Like Jesus' descent into hell, these doctrines allow room for interpretation. At its core, original sin affirms that we have somehow become alienated from God deep within our collective soul. Redemption, in turn, affirms that for any healing to take place Jesus must enter this realm of alienation and preach the Good News of God's love for every human being. When seen in this light, Jesus' descent into hell is the final stage of a process of his offering of self for the world's salvation. He has entered our world, given himself to us completely, to the point of dying for us, and even to the point of telling those who live in a state of complete alienation from the divine that God still loves them. Through the cross, Jesus reveals his message of divine compassion, breaks down the resistance of our primal alienation, and offers newness of life to all who would have it.

An example from Byzantine iconography illustrates this point very well. When depicting Jesus' "descent into hell," the artist normally depicts Jesus standing on the toppled gates of the underworld with a scroll in one hand and pulling Adam out of a deep bottomless pit with the other. Below Adam, angels are locking Satan and his dominions in chains that will hold them captive for all eternity. According to the principles of iconography, a scroll typically represents preaching the word. Since "Adam," in Hebrew, means "man" — in the universal sense of the term, what today many would refer to as "humanity" — Jesus' lifting of Adam, the first man, indicates the healing of humanity's primal wounds and its elevation to great heights through Christ's redeeming grace.[6]

The word preached by Jesus to those in hell boldly proclaims a new creation made possible by his rising from the dead. Through his resurrection, Jesus, the first fruit of the new humanity, takes fallen humanity by the hand, lifts it out of its state of alienation, and gives it the capacity to participate in a union with the divine more intimate than ever before thought possible. Jesus' descent among the dead cannot be properly understood apart from his rising from the dead. It relates to the resurrection as the doctrine of original sin relates to redemption. They, too, are like two sides of a coin: one depends on and cannot exist without the other.

From Hell to Deep Heaven

The choice of the phrase "alienation from the divine" as the existential equivalent to the Christian doctrine of hell has much in its favor. The term "alienation" is commonly used by many spiritual writers today and, when taken to its extreme, conveys a sense of the intense pain and isolation experienced in a life marked by a total absence of God. To those who have difficulties with such a teaching, C. S. Lewis has this to say:

> What are you asking God to do? To wipe out their past sins and at all costs to give them a fresh start, smoothing every difficulty and offering every miraculous help? But He has done so, on Calvary. To forgive them? They will not be forgiven. To leave them alone? Alas, I am afraid that is what He does.[7]

"The one principle of hell is — 'I am my own.' "[8] These words of George MacDonald, a nineteenth-century Scottish novelist, poet, and fantasy writer who was greatly admired by Lewis, remind us that there are some people who simply refuse to be converted. God refuses to force his love upon such people and, in the end, simply lets them be. "The characteristic of lost souls," Lewis says, "is 'their rejection of everything that is not simply themselves.' "[9]

The contrast between heaven and hell cannot be more apparent than here. Those in heaven center their lives on God and become more fully human; those in hell center their lives on themselves and end up losing themselves in the process. Lewis puts it this way:

> To enter heaven is to become more human than you ever succeeded in being on earth; to enter hell is to be banished from humanity. What is cast (or casts itself) into hell is not a man: it is "remains." To be a complete man means to have the passions obedient to the will and the will offered to God: to *have been* a man — to be an ex-man or "damned ghost" — would presumably mean to consist of a will utterly centered in its self and passions utterly uncontrolled by the will. It is, of course, impossible to imagine what the consciousness of such a creature — already a loose congeries of mutually antagonistic sins rather than a sinner — would be like. There may be a truth in the saying that "hell is hell, not from its own point of view, but from the heavenly point of view."[10]

Elsewhere, Lewis asserts that human beings have the capacity to dehumanize themselves, that is, to treat both themselves and others as mere objects. When that occurs, they become slavish prisoners in a lonely hell of their own making.[11] Jesus descends into hell to tell those who have alienated themselves completely from God and devolved into a conglomeration of their base animal instincts that he still loves them and wishes to lead them to the joys of Deep Heaven. He extends his mercy even to people such as these. This understanding of hell as "alienation from the divine" teaches us a number of important things about our own journey to the joy of Deep Heaven.

Through *the negative example of the alienated self*, it shows us what happiness is not and reminds us of the importance of living for something greater than ourselves. As such, it underscores the important role we play in deciding our destiny and reminds us that God will not reject us if we humbly turn to him and seek forgiveness.

It is *a stark reminder of what our lives would be like without Jesus*. God's crucified Son entered the realm of the dead in order to conquer death and raise us to new life. Without him, there would be no way to overcome our alienation from God and follow him on the way to Deep Heaven.

It tells us that *the ability to choose carries with it great responsibility*. Human freedom is both a precious gift and a dangerous peril. Actions done in freedom shape us into the people we become and lead us ultimately to a final destiny of our own choosing. Because we are free, it is possible for some of us simply to refuse God's offer to make us whole and to give us fullness of life.

It tells us that *God can offer forgiveness to us but cannot accept it for us*. The journey to Deep Heaven is possible only for those who open their hearts to God freely, receive forgiveness for their sins, and follow in his footsteps. For most of us, this journey takes a lifetime and continues even beyond death.

It tells us that Jesus' descent was not a single, one-time event, but *an ongoing process of his seeking to engage and overcome our own alienation from God*. Because his saving action occurred both in and out of time, Jesus continues to offer himself for us to this very day by descending into the throes of our own alienation from God in order to transform us and make of us a new creation.

It tells us that hell *is about our alienation not only from God, but also from ourselves and others.* Just as love for God and neighbor are intimately related, so too are hatred and alienation from God and neighbor. The journey to Deep Heaven is a communal enterprise with the family of believers known as the communion of saints.

It reminds us that our journey to Deep Heaven involves a difficult process through which *our lives become less centered on ourselves and more centered on God.* In doing so, we become more fully human. Happiness in Deep Heaven is possible only when we turn our hearts completely over to God and allow him to shape us into the people he has always envisioned us to be.

It gives us *a deeper insight into the Catholic doctrine of purgatory.* If hell is the state of being in which individuals have become so alienated from God that they can no longer open their heart to God's compassionate love, then purgatory represents that state of being where a person's alienated heart is still capable of being moved to conversion.

It reminds us that *God wishes everyone to be saved.* Jesus' descent into hell shows us that his invitation to lead us to Deep Heaven extends to everyone, even to those who, for whatever reason, have alienated themselves from God. God sends this invitation to everyone, even though he knows full well that some may not accept it.

It reminds us that *happiness is not something we construct through our own efforts, but a gift which we must humbly receive from God with open and empty hands.* We become alienated from God when our lives are so full of self-centered interests that there is no room left for God.

We may summarize the above insights as follows. The journey from hell to Deep Heaven goes from one spiritual extreme to another. According to C. S. Lewis, "we know much more about heaven than hell, for heaven is the home of humanity and therefore contains all that is implied in a glorified human life."[12] Hell, in his mind, is vastly different: "It is in no sense *parallel* to heaven: it is 'the darkness outside,' the outer rim where being fades away to nonentity."[13] Jesus' descent into hell is an attempt on his part to keep those he loves from slipping away forever into an existence of desolate and lonely darkness. He goes there to try to open hearts that are closed to him so that he might lead them out of darkness into the light of Deep Heaven.

Conclusion

Jesus' descent into hell is all about reaching out to the alienated. It is a way of speaking about Jesus' proclamation of the truth of his resurrection even to those who have completely shut themselves off from the divine love. Although his love for humanity was deep and plentiful, Jesus was well aware that not everyone would be ready to accept his message of forgiveness and intimate friendship with the divine. He experienced rejection during his public ministry and fully expected the same (if not worse) when he journeyed to the land of the dead after his gruesome and bloody death by crucifixion. This knowledge, however, did not prevent him from proclaiming his transforming message of God's love in the realm of the dead. On the contrary, it emboldened him all the more.

The whole point of this chapter is that the shadowy realm of the dead lies not in some dark, murky Sheol beneath the pillars of the earth, but deep in the confines of the human heart. Even today, Jesus goes there to proclaim his message, brings an end to our alienation from God, and points out the way to Deep Heaven. Although the message he preaches is a source of vexation to many, many whose hearts have not yet been completely hardened will listen to it and be moved to repentance.

In the final analysis, Jesus' descent into hell affirms that the Good News is destined to be proclaimed not just to all the ends of the earth, but to the heights and depths of reality itself, especially in the heights and depths of the human heart. "God is everywhere," as we learned from our penny catechism — even in hell! He is present not only by virtue of his power in keeping all things in being, but also by virtue of his word and the healing message of hope he carries to our fallen and alienated humanity.

Reflection Questions

1. What does the doctrine of Jesus' descent into hell mean to you? Do you interpret it literally? Do you dismiss it as mythic language tied to an outdated worldview? Do you try to translate it to speak to the contemporary experience of what it means to be alienated from oneself, from others, and from God?

2. Do you agree that there is a distinction between the language in which a teaching of the faith is couched and the underlying truth it seeks to express? If so, does such a distinction help you to look at your beliefs differently? How has it affected your understanding of Jesus' descent into hell?

3. In what ways have you experienced alienation in your life? Do you understand the factors that contributed to your feeling this way? Were you able to overcome this experience of alienation or has it continued to remain in some way? Do you believe that Jesus suffered and died in order to bring God's love to the alienated? Do you believe he suffered and died to carry God's love to you?

4. Does the interpretation of Jesus' descent into hell presented in this chapter give you any new insights into the Catholic teaching on hell? Does it give you any insights into the Catholic teaching on purgatory? What does it say about the nature of divine love? Is God's redeeming grace limited or plentiful?

5. Do you believe that Jesus continues to descend into hell to this day by reaching out to the alienated? Do you believe that you participate in this redemptive action whenever you reach out to the alienated in your midst? In what way are you the hands and arms of Jesus in the world today?

Praying for Deep Heaven

I long for you, Lord, and I long for Deep Heaven.

*I ponder the meaning of your descent into hell,
      and I see nothing but your steadfast desire
      to save all human beings from alienation and
      self-imposed loneliness.*

*Your love for us makes you reach out to all people,
      even those who have alienated themselves
      from you.*

*You died for all human beings, and the only thing
      that can separate us from your love is our own
      stubbornness and selfish egoism.*

*Thank you, Lord, for bringing your love to the
      darkest corners of the human heart.*

*Thank you for offering us all a message of plentiful
      redemption.*

*Thank you for reaching out to the outcast and
      marginalized.*

Thank you, Lord, and help me.

*Help me to ponder those areas of my life that I
      still keep back from you and that alienate me
      from you.*

*Help me to turn these areas over to you so that you
      might heal me and make me whole.*

*Help me to reach out to the poor, the outcast, the
      marginalized, the alienated, and the lonely in
      my midst.*

*Help me to bear your gentle, quiet presence to them
so that they might open their hearts to you and
receive you as a brother and a friend.*

*Help me to befriend the friendless, to love the
unloved, to bear hope to the hopeless.*

Chapter Four

Overcoming Death

A man really ought to say, "The Resurrection happened two thousand years ago" in the same spirit in which he says, "I saw a crocus yesterday." Because we know what is coming behind the crocus. The spring comes slowly down this way; but the great thing is that the corner has been turned. There is, of course, this difference, that in the natural spring the crocus cannot choose whether it will respond or not. We can. We have the power either of withstanding the spring, and sinking back into the cosmic winter, or of going on into those "high mid-summer pomps" in which our Leader, the Son of man, already dwells, and to which He is calling us. It remains with us to follow or not, to die in this winter, or to go on into that spring and that summer.
—C. S. Lewis, *God in the Dock*

THERE WAS A TIME in my life when I looked upon Jesus' resurrection from the dead as nothing but a fictitious tale concocted by a group of disillusioned disciples who could not accept the loss of their "would-be Messiah" and the shattering of their deepest hopes against the wood of a brutal Roman cross. Who else but someone with a fragile mind, weakened by intense mourning and verging on despair would create such an outlandish story as a means of escaping the hard, cold facts of Golgotha? The resurrection of Jesus was an attractive tale but one that was too good to be true. It was either true or false, and I tended to side with the latter.

I changed my opinion on this matter only after a heartrending self-examination that led me to a stark realization. C. S. Lewis puts it this way: "If the story is false, it is at least a much stranger story than we expected, something for which philosophical 'religion,' psychical research, and popular superstition have all alike failed to prepare us. If the story is true, then a wholly new mode of being has arisen in the universe."[1]

If God existed and was all-powerful, as I believed, then why couldn't he invite us to share in a "new mode of being"? Why couldn't the laws of nature be turned inside-out and life's predestined rendezvous with death be duly kept, yet ultimately reversed? Lewis tells us that the resurrection is the central theme of every early Christian sermon.[2] Either these early apostles were sadly deranged and deluded, or they had truly experienced the opening of "a new chapter in cosmic history."[3]

After much thought, prayer, and soul-searching, I began to place my hopes in the testimony of these early disciples and came to affirm that "Christ's achievement in rising from the dead was the first event of its kind in the whole history of the universe."[4] Jesus, I came to believe, endured death and overcame it in order to bring us the first fruits of a new creation and to show us the way to Deep Heaven. His resurrection from the dead became the central mystery of my faith. To my mind, it is precisely what one would expect from an eternal, all-powerful, and ever-loving God. It maintains continuity between our present bodily condition and our transformed state in the life to come. It outshines all other notions of the afterlife.

Metaphors of Resurrection

Metaphors for the resurrection abound in nature. Seeds must be buried in the earth and die before they sprout victoriously in the spring and bear fruit. Caterpillars weave cocoons around themselves and are gradually transformed into fluttering butterflies. Lizards, snakes, and other reptiles retreat into a low metabolic, death-like state during their months of hibernation only to awake in the spring from their long wintry sleep.

We ourselves undergo numerous biological transformations from the moment of conception to the time of death. We enter the light of day from the darkened constraints of our mother's womb. We take in food and drink and gradually change it into our own flesh and blood. We awake from sleep each morning ready to face the challenges ahead. These are but a few of the ways in which the book of creation provides us with pregnant and telling signs of the world to come.

According to C. S. Lewis, this pattern of death and rebirth is "a thing written all over the world." In his mind, "it is the pattern of all vegetable life and of all animal generation as well." This pattern is "there in Nature because it was there first in God."[5] His reason for stating so is clear: "A Nature which is 'running down' cannot be the whole story. A clock can't run down unless it has been wound up. Humpty Dumpty can't fall off a wall which never existed. If a Nature which disintegrates order were the whole of reality, where would she find any order to disintegrate?"[6] As with any book, however, it is necessary for us to look at the markings on the page in front of us and to translate them into meaningful words and sentences. If we fail to do so, we simply will not benefit from what the book of creation has to offer us.

Unfortunately, many of us have forgotten how to ponder the traces of the divine in the world around us. We have adopted too pragmatic a view toward life and have come to think that the earth's only purpose is to serve our bodily material needs. As a result, we have forgotten how to look for and to listen to what God might be trying to say to us through it. We have lost touch with the material world and somehow feel as though we can do what we wish with it. This attitude manifests itself in a variety of ways.

We litter, pollute, deforest, deplete, and deprive our environment of its rich resources. We put little if anything back. We alienate ourselves from the world and from our place in it. Because we fail to contemplate the simple everyday signs and wonders that surround us, we sink more readily into loneliness and isolation and become easy prey for the disturbing voices of doubt and uncertainty. Instead of thinking that the material world will reveal the beyond to us, we look upon it upon as a hindrance, as something that keeps us back from finding and developing our deepest human potential. We consider it a burden to be overcome, a chain that ties us down. We do not read the book of creation, because many of us do not even believe that it exists. Even if we did believe in it, we would not allow it to reveal to us anything further than some very general evidence for God's existence. Images and metaphors of the resurrection would be definitely out of the question.

We are an integral part of the world in which we live. Once we lose contact with it, we also begin to lose touch with ourselves, with others, and with God. Our failure to contemplate the world around us and to ponder the traces and vestiges of the beyond imprinted in it by God cannot help but have an effect on our relationships. With such a desacralized view of the world, it does not take long before we begin treating other people in a manipulative, dehumanizing, even brutal manner. We forget how to ponder their deep inner goodness and begin to think that we can use them for our own purposes. To tap the rich resources within us, we need to rekindle in our hearts the desire to ponder creation and to decipher the vast array of signs and symbols that it lays before us. If we do so with open and sincere hearts, we will be surprised at what we discover and have great cause for celebration.

Competing Narratives

At this stage in the history of Christianity, the question facing many of us is this: "How much are we really aware of that cause?" One would think that, for all that the resurrection has going for it as an idea of the afterlife, people would be flocking to Christianity in droves. The contrary, however, seems to be the case — at least in Western culture.

As our current fascination with Oriental religions, new-age mysticism, and the occult attests, belief in the resurrection no longer attracts as large a genuinely convinced group of believers as it once did. That is not to say that we outright reject the concept, let alone the fact, of Jesus' resurrection. It simply means that we accept it only half-heartedly and no longer allow it to shape the way we live our lives. We have learned how to go through the motions of the church's collective belief, while reserving the right to entertain our own eclectic thoughts on it and related matters. We remember the creed by rote and even recite it. For many of us, however, the words have lost their ability to muster in us any deep religious conviction. They fail to register in our hearts and a make little headway in the sea of relativities and uncertainties that clamor in our minds.

This state of affairs necessarily has an effect on the way we celebrate the feast of Easter itself. In the past, Christians could not contain their joy in their celebration of the Pasch. They were so taken with the mystery that the church felt an increasing need to set aside more and more days for celebrating the feast on its liturgical calendar. In the course of time, a single day for celebrating the entire paschal mystery gradually turned into a triduum and then into an entire octave.

The present season of Easter, the fifty days from the Easter Vigil to the feast of Pentecost, has its roots in the church's developing efforts to enable the faithful to ponder as many aspects of Christ's paschal mystery as possible. Today the church retains the fifty-day season, but many of us have long forgotten its purpose. Instead of pondering the various facets of the Christ event and seeking their relevance for us, we are content with allowing other narratives, both sacred and secular, to fill our imaginations and shape our lives. Today, the Easter narrative is just one of many vying for our attention, each with its own dramatic pull and power to sway the imagination. The influence any one of these narratives can have on our lives is enormous. When push comes to shove, it is difficult to say which we will ultimately allow to capture our hearts.

One such narrative that has been present in our culture for quite some time is that of "the American Dream." Most of us do not need an explanation of its particulars, for we know them already, perhaps all too well. From the moment we get up in the morning to the time we go to sleep, we are bombarded by the media with messages from all directions about what we need (and in most cases need to buy) to make our lives complete. The list gets larger and more expensive with every generation: a bigger house, another car, a tiled patio, an outdoor pool, expensive furniture, a place in the country to get away to, etc. We have listened to these messages for so long that we have actually become convinced that the quality of our lives depends on the things we possess.

As a result, we work extra long hours to make enough money so that we can buy the things that we are told we need to lead happy, productive lives. We work ourselves to the bone in order to live up to a very superficial standard of success. More often than not, we are too tired to enjoy our acquisitions when we finally manage to find some free moments in our very busy schedules. As time goes on, we find it increasingly more difficult to step off the accelerated treadmill our lives have become. In the end, our quick-paced lives spin badly out of control and our possessions end up taking possession of us. There is nothing wrong with having things, even nice things. Allowing them to be the measure our self-worth, however, is another matter altogether.

For most of us, this dream of material success in the land of opportunity seems to be much more deeply rooted in our value system than in the narrative of Jesus' passion, death, and resurrection. Both narratives touch extremely important sectors of our lives, and we have somehow convinced ourselves that they can coexist in a relative state of peace. Such a judgment, however, could not be further from the truth. The underlying values of one narrative are deeply at odds with those of the other. Jesus' words to the rich young man to sell his possessions and give to the poor (Mt 19:21) may not have been intended for everyone. The spirit that inspired them, however, has nothing at all to do with middle America's dogged attempt to "keep up with the Joneses."

Key Elements of the Easter Proclamation

Our only recourse in such a situation is to go back to square one. As hard as it may be for some of us to admit, the only way we can transcend the current confusion that these competing narratives have brought to our lives is to step back from them and try to listen to them all as if for the first time. The difficulty of this task should not be underestimated. Doing so will require a disciplined mind, a listening heart, and a great deal of honesty. Here we will limit ourselves to an exposition of the Easter narrative. I

hope that the following reflections on this pivotal dimension of the book of God's word will, in some way, help
us to get back in touch with the unrestrained joy of the
original Easter proclamation and find its special relevance
for our daily lives.

Passion and Death

To begin with, Jesus' resurrection makes sense only against
the backdrop of his passion and death. To try to explain
it away by concocting a story that he never really died but
somehow feigned death either through drugs or by sub-
stituting a look-alike for himself on the cross does not do
justice to what little we do know about the events of Good
Friday. It also demeans the significance of what Christians
believe about the resurrection. Although the exact date
is not known, most reputable historians agree that Jesus
was condemned to death by Pontius Pilate, the Roman
procurator of Palestine at the time, and then tortured and
summarily executed by his soldiers.

It is also generally agreed that there was a certain
degree of complicity in the action on the part of the Jewish high priest and Sanhedrin. For our present purposes,
we are not concerned with who killed Jesus or their precise reasons for doing so, but with the indisputable fact
of his suffering and death on the cross. We are also concerned with the effect his death had on his followers.
Many of them had seen in him the victorious, triumphant
figure who would liberate Israel from its political domination and herald in a new age of peace. They could not
understand Jesus' attempt to tell them otherwise.

When he failed to meet their expectations, they reacted
in a variety of ways. One of his closest followers betrayed

him (see Mk 14:43–46). Another denied he ever had anything to do with him (see Mk 14:66–72). Most of the others simply ran away (see Mk 14:50). Some remained faithful to him right to very end (see Mk 15:40–41).

At the time of his death, all of them were downcast in heart and spirit. His death had left a deep hole in their souls, an emptiness that could not be filled. They had loved Jesus very much and could not believe that his mission had ended in such dismal failure. Losing a loved one is difficult as it is; doing so in the midst of public shame and the breakdown of one's deepest hopes, even more excruciating. The events of Good Friday placed Jesus' disciples in a deep spiritual crisis. They were distraught, disillusioned, and afraid. Most of them had gone into hiding and were not about to come out soon. It was from people like these that the Easter proclamation "He is risen!" would first find the light of day.

The Resurrection Appearances

The tragic events of Good Friday gave way to the astonishing news of an empty tomb on Easter morning. The disappearance of Jesus' corpse from the freshly hewn sepulcher in which he had been laid after his death came as a surprise to everyone. Even then, there were those who sought a rational explanation for it. Matthew's Gospel tries to dispel rumors that the body was taken away by his followers by having the Jewish high priest go to Pilate and insist that he place a guard at the tomb to prevent such a scenario from ever taking place (see Mt 27:62–66). The Easter proclamation, however, is not merely about an empty tomb, but about the disciples' actual experience of Jesus, their Lord and Master, whom they had presumed dead.

Although the various Gospel accounts pertaining to these experiences are not historical in the strict sense of the term, they do contain a number of similarities that give us a vague indication of what was experienced. For example, when Jesus appeared to his disciples, he was not immediately recognized (see Lk 24:13–35; Jn 20:11–18). This indicates that the resurrection was not merely a resuscitation of a corpse, but that witnesses perceived Jesus differently, as living in some transfigured, glorified state. In any case, the Gospel accounts affirm that it was not merely Jesus' spirit or ghost that was experienced, but Jesus himself: body, soul, and spirit (see Jn 20: 24–29).

The underlying continuity between the earthly and glorified Jesus is a fundamental element of the Easter proclamation. All that Jesus was on earth, in other words, continued to exist in a transformed state and was experienced by his disciples in the resurrection appearances. These experiences were given to a number of his disciples — both women and men — and in a variety of places. According to Paul, as many as five hundred disciples experienced him at one time (see 1 Cor 15:1–11).

Just as startling as the appearances of Jesus himself was the transformation that took place in the lives of those who saw him. This timid and fearful group of followers boldly proclaimed what they had seen and did so in the face of ridicule, persecution, and death. The amazing conviction of the disciples after the Easter appearances is the best evidence we have that their experience of Jesus was real. These men and women were not unbalanced religious fanatics who could be easily influenced by mood swings and what could be suggested to them by simply their deep desire to believe. They were simple, practical people from all walks of life who knew who Jesus was and who testified with their lives that what they had seen and proclaimed was true.

The Ascension

According to the two-volume work known as the Gospel of Luke and the Acts of the Apostles, Jesus appeared to his disciples over the course of forty days and then ascended into heaven (see Lk 24:50–53; Acts 1:3). Mark, the earliest of the Gospels, says that Jesus "was taken up into heaven" after he revealed himself to the Eleven while they were at table (see Mk 16:19). The two other Gospel accounts do not give a specific timetable for when Jesus stopped appearing to them so that he could take his seat at the right hand of the Father.

Either they were not interested in determining a fixed time for when this occurred or, as is more likely the case, they wished to show its intrinsic relationship to the resurrection itself. For our purposes, the ascension has a variety of important complementary meanings.

In the first place, Jesus must leave his disciples in order to complete the saving action begun out of obedience to the Father's will. Jesus came among us for the salvation of the world. After his death and resurrection, it was only fitting that he should take up his proper place at the right hand of the Father. One might go so far as to say that his redemptive journey was not complete until he returned to the very place from where he started.

Second, the ascension underscores the transcendent character of the paschal mystery. In his transformed state,

Jesus appeared to his disciples on a number of occasions and, according to the gospel accounts, even ate with them (see Jn 21:1–12). He could do this because of the underlying continuity existing between his earthly and glorified states. At the same time, his kingdom was not of this world, but of the new creation which his passion, death, and resurrection ushers in. The ascension is a theological way of stating that Jesus was no longer bound by the limitations of time and space. Of its very nature, his glorified existence points to a world beyond. Because of him, we have been given a glimpse of that world and hope one day to journey to it.

Finally, Jesus ascended to the right hand of the Father so that he could send us his Spirit and be present to us in a new way. Sporadic appearances in his glorified state to his disciples during a short period after his resurrection do not compare with the virtually universal presence that becomes possible through the gift of the Spirit. Here, too, we see how one facet of the Christ event reveals another and is, in fact, intimately connected with it.

The Sending of the Spirit

According to the Acts of the Apostles, the Holy Spirit descends upon Jesus' disciples ten days after the ascension. In the Gospels of Matthew (see Mt 28:16–20) and John (see Jn 20:21–23), the gift of the Spirit is more directly connected with the resurrection appearances themselves and the commissioning of the apostles. In Acts, the commissioning of the apostles and the sending of the apostles seem to be separate. The former is linked to Jesus' final words before his ascension (see Acts 1:6–9), while the latter occurs ten days later on the Jewish feast of Pentecost when the Spirit manifests itself in tongues of fire and gives those who receive it the gift of tongues (see Acts 2:1–13).

Regardless of their differences, all of the accounts agree that the sending of the Spirit is a direct result of Jesus' resurrection and ascension into heaven and a means of empowering the apostles to baptize, forgive sins, and preach the Good News with boldness and conviction. Peter's discourse to the people of Jerusalem immediately after the Pentecost is but one example of the great power of the Spirit (see Acts 2:14–40).

The sending of the Spirit initiates the birth of the church, the body of Christ. The Spirit of Christ is the soul of this new, supernatural organism, while believers form its many and diverse members. Through baptism, the Spirit immerses us in Christ's death and resurrection. In this very simple and ordinary ritual, Christ's redemptive action extends through space and time. Christ is the sacrament of God; the church, the sacrament of Christ; the seven sacraments, those of the church. The Holy Spirit is the point of continuity uniting each of these various dimensions of sacramental action. A sacrament is an outward sign of invisible grace only because the Holy Spirit makes it so. Another name for the Holy Spirit, in fact, is "Uncreated Grace." Whatever graces we receive either directly from God or through the visible signs of the sacraments themselves come to us only in and through the Spirit.

The Eucharist

All of the various dimensions of the paschal mystery — Jesus' passion, death, resurrection, ascension, and the sending of the Spirit — converge in the Eucharist. This symbolic action of Jesus stands in marked continuity with the long tradition of Hebrew prophetic utterance.

Hosea's marriage to the faithless Gomer (see Hos 1:2–9), Jeremiah's symbols of the loincloth (see Jer 13:1–11) and the shattered wine jugs (see Jer 13:12–14), Ezekiel's making of bread from a single pot of wheat, barley, beans, lentils, millet, and spelt (see Ezek 4:9) and his mime of the emigrant (see Ezek 12:1–16) are all examples of the prophetic use of concrete material signs and actions to convey the message of Yahweh to his people. What is so often forgotten when interpreting these actions is that, as authentic utterances of the word of God, they actually bring into effect what they symbolize: God's word does not return in vain (see Isa 55:11).

In this respect, Jesus' breaking of the bread and drinking of the cup in the company of his disciples brings the reality of the paschal mystery into their midst. That is to say, before his actual death, Jesus makes present the redemptive effects of Good Friday in the bread and wine that he eats and drinks with his disciples. These effects culminate in his Easter rising, his ascension, and his sending of the Spirit. The entire Christ event, one might say, centers around the Eucharist.

One sees this historically in the sense that the Last Supper occurred before Jesus' passion, death, and resurrection, while our memorial celebrations of this sacred meal take place after it. One sees this also sacramentally, because the Eucharist actually effects what it symbolizes. It makes present, in other words, both the sacrifice of Calvary and the risen Lord himself who, having ascended to the right hand of the Father, is present to the believing community through the gift of his Spirit and the transformation of bread and wine into his body and blood. It is for this very reason that the Eucharist is considered the source and summit of the church's life.

It is also for this very reason that we are encouraged to celebrate the sacrament frequently and to encourage others to do so. Through the Eucharist we are nourished by Christ himself and have the opportunity to be more deeply incorporated into his paschal mystery. Taking part in it is the most intimate way that we, the people of God, can give thanks for the saving work accomplished for us in Christ.

The Relevance of the Resurrection

It would be tragic if the above exposition of the main elements of the Easter narrative were perceived as having only a vague, abstract relevance for our lives. On the contrary, both our present and future joy depend on these elements. C. S. Lewis puts it this way: "Most certainly, beyond all worlds, unconditioned and unimaginable, transcending discursive thought, there yawns forever the ultimate Fact, the fountain of all other facthood, the burning and undimensioned depth of the Divine Life. Most certainly also, to be united with that Life in the eternal Sonship of Christ is, strictly speaking, the only thing worth a moment's consideration."[7] The Easter narrative should have an immediate impact on our present life of faith. To discover what it is, however, we need to look at each of the elements discussed above and see what they reveal to us about the nature of our religious outlook.

For one thing, contemplating Jesus' suffering and death forces us to confront our attitudes toward loss and failure. This is a part of the Easter narrative that many of us would rather overlook or quickly pass over. We distance ourselves from Jesus' passion and death because we ourselves are afraid of pain, suffering, and ultimately death itself. But it is when we fail, not when we succeed, that our true character comes to the fore. It is the way we face failure at school, the loss of a job, betrayal by a friend, societal rejection or marginalization, an unexpected illness, the death of a loved one, our own impending death that tells us who we really are.

At such moments, we discover what is most meaningful to us, what we really believe in; we get in touch with our deepest, truest self. It is from the midst of loss and failure that we recognize our inner poverty and need to depend totally on the Lord. It is from the depths of defeat that we undergo an inner transformation and find the resilience of spirit that enables us to pick ourselves up and carry on. At times, we peer into ourselves and do not even recognize the person we have become, so strange, so new, we seem to ourselves. There comes a time when these appearances of our deeper self pass away. They have not disappeared, but have ascended from the depths of our soul into the light of our conscious awareness.

When this occurs, we become present to ourselves in a new way. We have become vital, spiritual persons who not only care for ourselves and others, but also cherish their relationship with God and the world that God has placed us in. We celebrate our newfound fellowship with ourselves, with others, with God, and with the world in any number of ways. Everything we do becomes an opportunity for giving thanks to the Lord for his many gifts.

Each one of us goes through our own very personal experiences of suffering, death, resurrection, ascension, spiritual renewal, and thanksgiving. These moments are not unrelated to the Christ event, but are rather intimately a part of it. They remind us of the deepest realities of our lives and what penetrates the fabric of daily experience. They suggest that, even now, we are deeply wound up in the mystery of Christ. They tell us that what we hope for is taking place in our lives at this very moment. They encourage us to peer into the depths of our experience and find there the drama of the paschal mystery in a very concrete way. They remind us that the deep joy of heaven will be tailor-made for each of us, that, in the words of C. S. Lewis, "God will look to every soul as its first love because He is its first love."[8]

Conclusion

Christianity tells us that the death and resurrection of Jesus not only happened, but is also taking place in us, the members of his body. Unfortunately, many of us have a hard time finding the immediate relevance of this bedrock doctrine of our faith. The reason for this has to do with our inability to find a concrete link between the major elements of the Easter narrative and our daily experience.

This has been complicated by our changing relationship with the physical world and our increasing lack of interest (some might say "indifference") to the various signs and symbols present to us in the book of creation. The Easter proclamation is a joyful narrative, one that tells us that we

have reached an important turning point in the history of
the world, the beginning of a new creation. It is the place
where the book of creation and the book of the Word
come together and ultimately merge. The point of this
convergence is our own lives.

When we look within our hearts and ponder what we
find there, we eventually come upon a faint but lasting
reflection of Jesus' paschal mystery. In that reflection, we
come to see that our present struggle between life and
death has already taken place in the drama of the cross.
That drama opens up to us a deeper dimension of life,
one that we have never experienced before. Jesus' death
on the cross reveals to us the power of love in our struggle
against death. It shows us to what lengths love is willing
to go for the renewal of the human heart. It tells us that
the new creation of Spirit and Truth is inscribed in our
hearts and will never die.

It will never die, because Jesus will not allow it. Belief in
the risen Lord comes from him in order to draw us gradually back to him. It keeps alive in us the joyful hope that
our lives will not end in death, but will merely change.
It helps us to look forward to a transformed existence,
one in continuity with our present lives. It encourages
us to sustain a prayerful response to the contemporary
challenges of Christian discipleship, especially at our celebration of the Eucharist. It forms the basis upon which
life in the resurrection is anticipated in the present, thus
enabling us to live each moment to the fullest. It offers all
of this to us and promises to do very much more.

It is up to us, however, to open our hearts to the Lord
and allow his Spirit to effect its gentle, transforming work
in us. If we do not cooperate in this way, we will gradually

lose sight of Deep Heaven and fail to tap into our deepest human potential.

Reflection Questions

1. Do you think belief in the resurrection has lost its grip on the imagination of Western civilization? Has it lost its grip on you? How firmly do you believe in this foundational affirmation of the Christian faith? Would you be willing to die for it?

2. Is belief in the resurrection of the body just too good to be true? Is that why many today are opting for spiritual interpretations of the afterlife that overlook the body completely? Do you believe that your body is a constituent dimension of human existence?

3. What, to your mind, are the key elements of the Easter proclamation? Do you agree with the ones listed in this chapter? Is there anything you would add or detract from the list? Which element would you emphasize the most?

4. How does resurrection relate to the cross? Is it possible to have one without the other? Does one necessarily lead to the other? What crosses are you presently carrying in your daily life? Do you have any hope in overcoming them? What is the relationship between resurrection and hope?

5. What is the relevance of the resurrection for your life today? Does your belief in the resurrection affect your outlook on life? Does it affect the way you live your life? Would you be living your life any differently if you did not believe in the resurrection?

Praying for Deep Heaven

I long for you, Lord, and I long for Deep Heaven.

I ponder the empty tomb and stand in awe of the power that topples death.

It seems almost too good to be true to believe that you overcame death and promise to do the same for me.

I admit, Lord, that I am not thoroughly convinced by your message of hope.

I admit that I am full of doubts and that the fear of dying has an inordinate hold over me. I find myself both believing and disbelieving. I long to hope that I too might one day overcome death, yet something still pulls me back from committing myself totally.

Thank you, Lord, for accepting my meager attempts at faith, themselves your gift.

Thank you, Lord, and help me.

Help me to overcome my fear of death.

Help me to believe in your resurrection and the hope of mine with all my heart, mind, soul, and strength.

Help me to live totally for the fullness of life that is to come.

Help me to keep my gaze focused firmly on the transformation you promise to work in me.

Help me to live my life in the light of what I hope it will one day become.

Thank you for conquering death for me, Lord.

Help me to trust in your promises.

Chapter Five

Returning Home

The "Resurrection" to which they bore witness was, in fact, not the action of rising from the dead but the state of having risen; a state, as they held, attested by intermittent meetings during a limited period (except for the special, and in some ways different, meeting vouchsafed to St. Paul). This termination of the period is important, for, as we shall see, there is no possibility of isolating the doctrine of the Resurrection from that of the Ascension.
— C. S. Lewis, *Miracles*

I'VE NEVER BEEN THERE, but I am told that under the center dome of the Chapel of the Ascension on the Mount of Olives, the highest point in Jerusalem, a footprint in a stone marks the exact place where Jesus ascended into heaven. Down through the centuries, pilgrims the world over have gone to this curious relic to venerate it and see for themselves the precise place where the risen Lord ended his earthly sojourn and returned to the right hand of his Father in heaven. Whatever its actual historical value, whenever I think of this simple stone imprint I cannot help but picture in my mind Jesus intently blasting off into the clouds to give his disciples one final display of his miraculous and majestic power. After all, how else could he have left such a deep and lasting impression in a slab of solid rock?

At times like these, the cynic in me comes alive and seriously objects to the above scene. He tells me that the opening description in Acts of the Apostles of Jesus being lifted up in a cloud and taken up into heaven before his disciples' eyes pushes the historical credibility of the gospel message to the limit. I wonder about what his disciples witnessed. What actually took place? What did they see?

The scriptures give only a few descriptions of Jesus' ascension, and scholars generally agree that two of them come from the same hand (Lk 24:50–53; Acts 1:4–11). I wondered why most of New Testament writers seem silent about it. Do they simply take it for granted? Do they imply it? Are they silent because it did not happen? If not, then what actually *did* take place? What is the precise relationship between Jesus' ascension and his resurrection from the dead? What relevance, moreover, does it have for me and my own spiritual journey?

Every story has a beginning and an end. Jesus' ascension cannot be understood apart from his resurrection. His ascent into heaven completes his selfless outpouring on our behalf and tells us something very important about human existence. Also, to understand the full significance of his ascension, we must look at Jesus' relationship both to the Father and to ourselves. This dual relationship stems from the close union of God and man in Jesus and makes possible our own journey to the Father and the joy of Deep Heaven. Without it, we would never be able to rise above our sinful humanity and be lifted up to an intimate union with the divine.

Returning to the Father

As Christians we are not bound to what C. S. Lewis calls the "primitive crudities" of the ascension story: "the vertical ascent like a balloon, the local Heaven, the decorated chair to the right of the Father's throne."[1] At the same time, he insists that we can drop the ascension story altogether "only if we regard the Resurrection appearances as those of a ghost or hallucination. For a phantom can just fade away; but an objective entity must go somewhere — something must happen to it."[2]

If we wish to proclaim that Jesus truly rose from the dead and that he exists transformed — body, soul, and spirit — in a new mode of being, then it is important for us to affirm his bodily ascension into heaven. Without it, the story of Jesus' paschal mystery remains incomplete, and his Risen Life becomes "a life without space, without history, without environment, with no sensuous elements in it."[3] Jesus' resurrection, in other words, was not merely a "spiritual" ("nonmaterial") happening, but involved a thorough transformation of every dimension of his human makeup.

Jesus can ascend into heaven only because he first descended to earth. He descended from heaven for our sake and returns for the same reason. The doctrine of the ascension affirms the elevated status of Jesus' humanity and holds out to us the hope of our own future glory. This is so because Jesus ascends to the Father to become king of a new creation and head of a new humanity.

His glorified humanity binds us to him and him to us. Through his ascension, Jesus completes his lifesaving journey and regains his rightful place at the Father's right hand, where he continuously intercedes for us as priest, prophet, and king.

The Gospels tell us that Jesus' kingdom is both "in our midst" yet "not of this world" (see Luke 17:21; Jn 18:36). The tension between these two seemingly contradictory statements reveals the enigmatic character of Jesus' message. His ascension affirms the truth of his message but also reveals its mysterious contours in the heart of God. The descriptive nature of the Gospel accounts requires a presentation of Jesus ascending into heaven within the historical boundaries of time and space (see Lk 24:51; Acts 1:9–10). Like Jesus' resurrection, however, to which it is intrinsically bound, the ascension bursts through these dimensions and ultimately transcends them.

Jesus is the Lord of history who came to make all things new; he now sits at the right hand of the Father as king of the new heaven and the new earth, realities existing both in and out of time. Jesus' ascension is not a "historical event" in the typical sense of the phrase; it happened more outside of time and space than in it. For this reason, it conceals as much as it reveals, carrying with it an aura of glory that far exceeds our powers of comprehension. In the midst of this uncertainty, all we can do is trust in Jesus' promise that, once lifted up, he will draw all of humanity to himself (see Jn 12:32).

As Christians, we believe that Jesus ascended into heaven so that we might one day join him. If this is so, then the true meaning of the ascension has a great deal to do with seeing God and our inability to do so on our own. The ascension is about our incapacity to see God and Jesus' power to grant us this sight. We can hope to see God face-to-face only because Jesus, our saving Lord, this very moment lives in the Father's presence and mediates divine life to us through the gift of his Spirit.

Without Jesus' return to the Father, there would be little room for hope and much reason to doubt. Jesus ascends into heaven, because the Father has called him home and, through him, us as well. He has gone there to stand in the Father's presence and prepare a place where we too can enjoy intimate fellowship with the divine (see Jn 14:2). "The ascension," C. S. Lewis reminds us, "belongs to a New Nature."[4] It reminds us that we now share in Jesus' transformed humanity and that, through him, God the Father at this very hour is calling us to his side.

Christ's Saving Mission

The "vision of God" (*visio Dei*) is another name for this intimate relationship with God. It can be taken in two ways: "God's vision of us" or "our vision of God," with the latter typically known as the "beatific vision." Jesus' ascension to the right hand of the Father affects each of these understandings. Because of the ascension, God gazes upon us through the prism of Jesus' glorified humanity, a specific fruit of his divine self-offering. Through his saving mission, Christ heals and elevates our fallen humanity, allowing us to share once more in the fullness of divine life. Jesus' ascension gives glory to God by making it possible for us to become fully alive by experiencing anew a life of intimate communion with the divine. In doing so, it presupposes every other aspect of his saving mission and ultimately brings it to completion.

What are the key features of this mission? For one thing, the undertaking both begins and ends in the divine. In much the same way as a lifeguard dives into deep water to save a drowning victim, God's Word enters our world in order to rescue us from the raging waters of our helplessness and inner brokenness. Christ suffers and dies to cleanse our wounds, resuscitate us, and ultimately transform us; he embraces our human situation in its entirety.

To do so, he must plumb the depths of human suffering, enter the darkness of the human heart, and commend his human spirit to the care of God. This downward movement into the depths of humanity's inner self-alienation represents Christ's purgative journey on our behalf. It is the necessary prelude for his "rising from the dead," which brings about the healing and transformation of our broken humanity and his "ascension into heaven." A lifeguard enters the water with the hope of rising out of it with the person he wished to save. In a similar way, this divine "descent" into the depths of our humanity ends in Christ's exalted "ascent" to the right hand of the Father and our sharing in his divine life as members of his glorious body.

The above description of Christ's saving mission highlights its liberating effects on our human condition. Jesus' ascension into heaven represents that aspect of his paschal mystery that restores his divinity to its proper place of honor and brings his glorified humanity into the presence of the Father. We, in turn, follow Jesus. As members of his body, the church, our humanity — body, soul, and spirit — is intimately bound to his. Jesus' ascension into heaven is thus a prelude to our own ultimate transformation and ascent into glory. This is true especially since his return to the Father releases the power of his Spirit upon the community of believers and initiates the church's sacramental and sanctifying mission through time.

The Dynamics of Prayer

What does this mean for our practical, day-to-day experience? To understand the relevance of Jesus' ascension for us today, we must once again draw a distinction between the expression itself and the truth it seeks to convey. The signal to stop at a crossroads can be communicated to the driver of a car in any number of ways: through a stop sign, a stop light, or a police officer — to name but a few. Something similar holds true for the teachings of the faith.

If we are not careful, the term "ascension" can easily lock us into a three-dimensional frame of mind and lead us to draw a much too facile picture of Jesus blasting off from earth to some unknown destination beyond the clouds. C. S. Lewis reminds us that even the New Testament writers "never thought merely of a blue sky or merely of a 'spiritual' heaven. When they looked up at the blue sky they never doubted that there, whence light and heat and the precious rain descended, was the home of God: but on the other hand, when they thought of one ascending to that Heaven they never doubted He was 'ascending' in what we would call a 'spiritual sense.' "[5] We too must recognize that the mystery of Jesus' ascension is much more than the concepts and images we use to express it.

While there may very well have been some historical dimension to Jesus' ascension, we have seen that the deeper meaning of the doctrine has something to do with how Jesus' return to the Father completes his saving mission and reestablishes our capacity to share in God's life. This insight gains even more weight when we realize that, as part of the paschal mystery, Christ's ascension transcends history, touches the eternal, and enables us to do the same.

Because of the ascension and all it represents, Christ's Spirit is sent forth to breathe divine life into us and offer us a share in the life of the Trinity. The Spirit makes us a holy people, gives us access to the church and its sacraments, and, most importantly, enables us to develop an intimate relationship with God through prayer. Could there be a relationship between the dynamics of prayer and those of Christ's saving mission, especially as manifested in his ascension into heaven and its Pentecostal aftermath? There is evidence to suggest that there is.

In his book *Pray without Ceasing,* Fabio Giardini identifies some of the underlying dynamics of Christian prayer.[6] Prayer *ascends* by allowing a person to lift his or her mind and heart to God and then *address* God as other. This understanding of prayer concentrates on the attitudinal posture of the believer at prayer. Rather than starting with God and studying the influence of divine grace on the individual, it presupposes this activity and chooses instead to look at the interior dispositions of the person praying. In doing so, it becomes clear that authentic Christian prayer involves an upward, rising motion toward the divine and an attempt to converse with it.[7]

Prayer as *worship* and *communion,* by way of contrast, represents the added attempt on the part of the believer to establish and maintain an authentic rapport with God. *Worship* highlights the creator-creature relationship between the person and God. It manifests itself in acts of petition, intercession, thanksgiving, praise, and adoration. *Communion,* in turn, focuses on the intimate friendship between the person at prayer and God made possible by Christ's saving mission. It manifests itself in benevolence, reciprocity, and an experience of mutual indwelling.[8]

Giardini affirms the importance of a thorough integration of these various dimensions of prayer. They are like streams that converge into a single river: "Prayer as *ascent* and as *address* offer praying Christians the first opportunity of getting acquainted with God. Prayer as *worship* and as *communion* brings about and develops an interpersonal relationship characterized by the reverence and intimacy of praying Christians with God."[9]

One way to see these various dimensions of prayer together at work would be to picture in your mind a man at prayer. Watch him as he raises his head and heart to God (*ascent*), opens his mouth (*address*), speaks words of adoration, praise, thanksgiving, and petition (*worship*), and enjoys a sense, however fleeting, of resting in God's presence (*communion*). The more he prays in this manner, the more will these various dimensions of prayer, while remaining distinct, instill in his heart a deep and abiding attitude of prayerfulness. This "loving awareness of God's presence" comes about by repeatedly opting to live in union with God and takes root beneath the level of a person's conscious awareness.[10] Even though these dimensions eventually converge in the action of prayer, a clear understanding of the differences between them can be very helpful. This is especially true for our understanding the relevance of the doctrine of Christ's ascension.

The Ascension and Christian Prayer

As pointed out earlier, the ascension tells us something about our incapacity to see God and Jesus' power to overcome death and lead us to the fullness of life and the joy of Deep Heaven. In the words of C. S. Lewis: "Christ has ascended into Heaven. And in due time all things, quite strictly all, will be subjected to Him. It is He who having been made (for a while) 'lower than the angels,' will become the conqueror and ruler of all things, including death and (death's patron) the devil."[11] Another way of saying this is that the ascension represents the final act in the drama of Christ's saving mission, which reopens the lines of communication between the human and the divine. After he ascends to the Father, Jesus can finally send his Spirit to the community of believers and endow us with the power to worship in spirit and in truth (see Jn 4:23–24). Why must he ascend to the Father before sending his Spirit to his disciples? The various dimensions of prayer discussed above offer some important insights.

In finding an explanation, it is important to note that Jesus, the God-Man, ascends to the Father in his glorified humanity and definitively reestablishes the intimate fellowship between the human and the divine lost by humanity's primal fall from grace. By focusing on this important role of Jesus' glorified humanity, we are able to understand the intimate relationship between Jesus' *ascent* into heaven and the corresponding *descent* of the Holy Spirit.

To see how this is so, keep that picture of the man at prayer in your mind. Remember as you see him raise his head and open his mouth that the dimensions of *ascent* and *address* represent the underlying attitudes of someone trying to establish contact with the divine. Remember, too, as he speaks words of adoration, praise, thanksgiving, and petition and experiences a sense of God's presence that *worship* and *communion* pertain to the personal bonds forged through the continual and deepening action of prayer.[12] While valuable in itself, this metaphor and the underlying dynamics it reveals also help us understand the relevance of Jesus' ascension for prayer and the spiritual life. Jesus, one might say, raises his head as he ascends to the Father (*prayer as ascent*) and then opens his mouth to intercede with him on our behalf (*prayer as address*). The resulting outpouring of the Holy Spirit enables the community of believers to give praise and glory to God (*prayer as worship*) and then experience union with God and one another (*prayer as communion*). In this way, Jesus' prayer becomes our own. It should not surprise us that the inner dynamics of prayer resemble those involved in Jesus' ascension and the descent of the Spirit. Jesus' saving mission and the sanctifying mission of his Spirit provide the pattern for these dynamics. Nor should it surprise us that these same dynamics also reveal something telling about the joy of Deep Heaven.

Ascent

When Jesus ascends to the right hand of the Father, he carries with him his glorified humanity. For C. S. Lewis, the ascension thus represents not only a great act of God, but also "the triumph of Man."[13] Healed of its tragic flaws and elevated to new heights, human nature once more enters the presence of God. The prayerful ascent of a renewed humanity enables us once more to enter into intimate fellowship with the divine. This glorified humanity, however, is Jesus' personal possession and ours only as an unrealized potential planted deep within our hearts. To receive any benefit from it, its fruits must come to us both as individuals and as a community of believers at some time during our historical sojourn. To enable this to happen, Jesus intercedes with the Father on our behalf and opens the way for us to ascend to God through his glorious humanity. The joy of Deep Heaven flows from this glorious human ascent, which Jesus makes possible by empowering us through his powerful intercession *to lift up* our hearts and minds to God in prayer.

Address

Intercessory prayer asks God for something on behalf of someone else. As a form of address, it aptly describes Christ's prayer for humanity at the right hand of the Father. Jesus "is the one intercessor with the Father on behalf of all men, especially sinners."[14] He intercedes in and through his glorified humanity, which ascends into heaven with Christ and joins him as he addresses God as Father. In this way, Christ restores humanity's capacity for intimate dialogue with God, and the bond of love he shares with the Father can now pour itself out on the rest of humanity.

Christ's intercession for us with the Father makes possible the gift of his Spirit and empowers us through the gift of faith not only to address God once more as Father, but also to worship him in spirit and in truth. "What is more natural, and easier," C. S. Lewis asks us, "if you believe in God, than to address Him? How could one not?"[15] The joy of Deep Heaven flows from Christ giving us the gift of his Spirit, which enables us *to address* God as "Abba, Father."

Worship

Worship is the act of giving praise and adoration to God. The indwelling of the Holy Spirit, which follows the ascension of Jesus' glorified humanity and his intercession for us with the Father, enables us to render spiritual sacrifices of praise and thanksgiving. The act of worship underscores the creator-creature relationship, which humanity denied early on in its origins by succumbing to the inordinate desire to "be like gods" (see Gen 3:5).

Through his divine self-offering, Jesus enables us to walk once more in fellowship with the Father, this time as his adopted sons and daughters. To do so, it is important for us to keep the boundaries clear between the supernatural and the natural. C. S. Lewis reminds us that "one must learn to walk before one can run."[16] We can walk in fellowship with God only if we recognize that we have been created in his image and likeness. The Spirit of Christ dwelling within our hearts reminds us of this fundamental relationship and enables us to render true worship to God with all our heart, mind, soul, and strength. The joy of Deep Heaven flows from Jesus' enabling us *to worship* God, our Creator, precisely in this way.

Communion

God has created us not merely to be his creatures, but to live in intimate friendship with him. The indwelling of the Holy Spirit made possible by Jesus' ascent and intercession with the Father on our behalf enables us not only to worship God in spirit and in truth, but also to commune with him on every level of our being. Rooted in benevolence, reciprocity, and mutual indwelling, this friendship with God is a reflection of the love within the Trinity itself. Jesus' ascent into heaven and the Holy Spirit's subsequent descent into and indwelling in our hearts represents God's drawing humanity into the heart of his divine love.

We can live in communion with God only because Jesus has rescued us by entering our world, becoming one of us, suffering for us, laying down his life for us, rising from the dead, and ascending into heaven. This saving mission makes it possible for us to receive the gift of the Spirit and live in intimate union with God. "To put ourselves ... on a personal footing with God," C. S. Lewis reminds us, "could, in itself and without warrant, be nothing but presumption and illusion. But we are taught that it is not; that it is God who gives us that footing. For it is by the Holy Spirit that we cry 'Father.' "[17] When seen in this light, the joy of Deep Heaven flows from our capacity *to commune* with God the Father made possible though our intimate relationship with Christ's Spirit.

An integration of these inner dynamics of prayer eventually develops into an attitude of prayerfulness, which represents our continual option for the value of living in communion with God.[18] In the same way, Jesus' ascension and intercession with the Father on our behalf, while always remaining distinct, unites with the worship of the church on account of the communion of its members with Christ's glorified humanity. Through its liturgical worship, the body of Christ raises it head and heart to God (*ascent*), opens its lips to proclaim Christ's gospel of love (*address*), speaks words of adoration, praise, thanksgiving, and petition (*worship*), and experiences a deep sense of unity with God (*communion*).

The Holy Spirit indwelling in Christ's glorified humanity is the point of convergence of these various dimensions of God's plan for humanity. The Spirit is with Christ as he ascends to the Father and intercedes with him on our behalf. The Spirit *descends* only because Christ *ascends*. The Spirit worships the Father within our hearts only because Christ himself addresses the Father for us on our behalf. The Spirit communes with us only because it first communes with Christ and the Father. Although inexorably distinct, the mysteries of Christ's ascent into heaven and the descent of the Holy Spirit are also intimately tied.

Rooted in Jesus' glorified humanity, they are like two sides of the same coin: one exists because of the other; their common purpose is the redemption of our humanity and the ongoing process of sanctification flowing from it. In the words of C. S. Lewis, through Christ's ascension and the descent of the Holy Spirit, we "assume the high rank of persons" before God who, in turn, descends to us and "becomes a Person to us."[19]

Conclusion

According to C. S. Lewis, Jesus' ascension into heaven is an essential truth of the Christian faith: "You cannot take ... it ... away without putting something in its place."[20] The whole point of this chapter has been that this Christian teaching is not some arcane mythological construct rooted in a worldview foreign to our own with little or no relevance for our daily lives, but a foreshadowing of our ultimate journey into God's very presence.

As such, it offers some important insights into how this process of our becoming holy and "god-like" takes shape within our lives. To understand its significance, it is important to see its relationship to what comes both before and after it.

Jesus' ascension to the right hand of the Father is but a single dimension of his overall saving mission, which includes his divine self-offering in the mysteries of his incarnation, life and ministry, passion, death, and resurrection. The specific role it plays in the overall scheme of God's providential plan for us is to mark both the conclusion of the saving mission of the Son and the beginning of the sanctifying mission of the Holy Spirit. Jesus' ascension actually foreshadows the Spirit's sanctifying mission: the movements of *ascent* and *address* of Jesus' glorified humanity parallel those of *worship* and *communion* within the Spirit-inspired community of believers.

In the life of prayer, the actions of *ascent, address, worship,* and *communion* ultimately merge to form a stream of unceasing prayer manifested in the deeply rooted attitude of prayerfulness in the life of believers. These dimensions of prayer, however, are themselves nothing but a reflection of the underlying dynamics in the immanent life and actions of God, especially as revealed in Christ's ascent to the Father and his Spirit's descent upon his followers.

The freeing and liberating pattern of Christ's ascension and the descent of his Spirit has imprinted itself on the prayer life of the community of believers and — as evidenced by the stone imprint in the Chapel of the Ascension in Jerusalem atop the Mount of Olives — in the Christian imagination as well. Christ continually ascends with the church at prayer and pours out his Spirit upon it as it celebrates his paschal mystery. He does so especially at the Eucharist, when as members of his body, we commune with him, approach the threshold of Deep Heaven, and receive a foretaste of the mysterious wonders and joys yet to come.

Reflection Questions

1. Why did Jesus have to return to the Father? What role does his ascension into heaven play in his overall saving mission? Is it essential to that mission or merely ancillary?

2. Does Jesus' ascension into heaven reveal anything to you about the spiritual life? Do you see any parallels between it and the dynamics of Christian prayer? If Jesus ascends to the Father, in what way do the members of his body do so?

3. Does the connection between Jesus' ascension into heaven and the operational dimensions of prayer — ascent and address — make sense to you? Does this connection show you how prayer can be considered "the great means of salvation" (St. Alphonsus)? What does it tell you about the nature of prayer?

4. Does the connection between Jesus' ascension into heaven and the relational dimensions of prayer — worship and communion — make sense to you? In what ways is Jesus' ascension a preparation for the way the members of his body relate to the Father? Does it tell you anything about your own life of prayer?

5. In what sense is Jesus still returning to the right hand of the Father through the prayers of his followers? In what sense is he not? What do we mean when we say that the members of Jesus' body genuinely participate in his paschal mystery? How does this apply to his ascension into heaven? How does this apply to you?

Praying for Deep Heaven

I long for you, Lord, and I long for Deep Heaven.

When I ponder your return in glory to your Father's right hand, I think of all you accomplished to reach this point and all that will happen as a result of it. You have returned home, Lord. You are where you belong.

Your ascension into heaven teaches me not only about you, but also something about myself, about my deepest hopes and dreams.

It stirs in me a desire to accompany you, to return home with you, to sit with you at your Father's side. The word of the Lord has not returned in vain.

Your return to the Father has made possible my own journey home.

Through your death and resurrection, you have invited me to join you at his side as a member of your body. Because of you, Lord, only because of you am I able to sit in the presence of the Father as an adopted child.

Thank you, Lord, for carrying me home.

Thank you for loving me so.

Please help me. Help me to nourish this relationship I share with you.

Help me to worship and commune with the Father.

Help me to serve him, and you, and the Spirit well.

Help me to carry others the way you have carried me.

Help me to be a worthy citizen of Deep Heaven.

Chapter Six

Longing for Deep Heaven

There are many reasons why the modern Christian and even the modern theologian may hesitate to give to the doctrine of Christ's Second Coming that emphasis which was usually laid on it by our ancestors. Yet it seems to me impossible to retain in any recognizable form our belief in the Divinity of Christ and the truth of the Christian revelation while abandoning, or even persistently neglecting, the promised, and threatened, Return. "He shall come again to judge the quick and the dead," says the Apostles' Creed. "This same Jesus," said the angels in Acts, "shall so come in like manner as ye have seen him go into heaven." "Hereafter," said our Lord himself..., "shall ye see the Son of Man... coming in the clouds of heaven."

— C. S. Lewis, *The World's Last Night*

W HEN I WAS A CHILD I thought of heaven as God's home in the sky. It was a place of white clouds and bright lights, where everyone was happy and no one cried. Heaven was the place where good people went after they died. God looked over your life and decided if you had been good enough to share his home. I wanted to pass his test (didn't everyone?), but wasn't quite sure if I would. I also wondered what it would be like spending eternity floating around on a cloud. What would there be to do there?

There was a part of me that was afraid I might get bored. How could I be happy without running around on the ground, breaking a sweat, and getting my hands dirty? Yes, I certainly had some reservations about heaven, but what other option was there? My choices were rather limited. Whatever it was, hell absolutely, positively *had* to be worse, while purgatory was a relatively short-lived postponement of one's home in the clouds. Faced with the necessity of choice and few alternatives, I continued asking God to take me to heaven when my time came, more by default than out of genuine interest.

Deep Heaven is very different from my childhood musings on life after death. It is full of risk and adventure, a state of existence that brings out our full potential and challenges us to journey ever deeper into the mystery of the divine. In one respect, however, it reflects at least one important element of my childhood idea of the hereafter — belief in a final judgment. It is a simple truth of the Catholic faith that each of us must give an account of our life before God and accept the happy (or dire) consequences of our actions.

Our faith tells us that Jesus Christ will return at the end of time in order to judge the world and establish the fullness of his kingdom.[1] Probably no other belief has held such powerful sway over the Catholic imagination over the years as the doctrine of the last judgment. We need only to picture the foreboding scene of Michelangelo's *Last Judgment* that adorns the Sistine Chapel to get a sense of the cataclysmic upheaval of time and space awaiting us at the world's end.

Each Sunday we gather for worship and proclaim aloud: "He will come again in glory to judge the living and the dead, and his kingdom will have no end."[2] These words from the Nicene Creed remind us that human history is not open-ended, but limited, finite, and drawing to a close. They also remind us that our happiness (or lack thereof) ultimately depends on the choices we make in life. Just how this final reckoning will take place is not for us to say. The Gospels themselves remind us of this very important truth: "But about that day or hour no one knows, neither the angels in heaven, nor the Son, but only the Father" (Mk 13:32).

The Depths of Faith

This lack of knowledge concerning the day or hour of our Lord's coming should affect the way we think and live in the present. It bids us to savor each moment of time as if it might be our last. It also encourages us to take a good look at our lives and to put things in their proper perspective. Conversion, we are told, must be ongoing. While we normally apply this insight to the moral dimensions of our faith, we also need to recognize its significance for even more basic teachings. The importance of this statement becomes all the more clear when we recognize the intimate relationship between how we act and what we affirm about the nature of reality.

If a gap exists between what we say with our lips and what we truly believe in our hearts, then there will most likely be a corresponding gap between the moral principles we publicly profess as a body of believers and the actual way we lead our lives. In the context of the church's teaching on the last judgment, we need to ask ourselves how deeply we believe in and are attached to it. Has our belief in it deepened over the years or diminished? Do we ever think about its meaning? Does this belief mediate truth to us? Does it make sense to us anymore? Does it inform our lives in any way? Or do we look upon it as a doctrinal holdover from a former age with little relevance for our present time, one that is best dealt with by giving it minimal notional assent or, worse yet, by simply ignoring it?

If we are honest, most of us would have to admit that our outward actions do not always do justice to the implications of the doctrine of the last judgment. We say we believe it (and we do, but only half-heartedly). The teaching has little, if any, real bearing on the way we live our lives. We cannot explain exactly why this is so.

Here we may be reminded of H. Richard Niebuhr's somber assessment of late nineteenth-century Protestant liberal theology: "A God without wrath brought men without sin into a kingdom without judgment through the ministrations of a Christ without a cross."[3] Niebuhr's statement hits home. It touches an aspect of our ongoing predicament of faith and, we may assume, that of many others. It reflects a hidden, subliminal message that holds great sway over us and that, much to our dismay, we find ourselves actually backing up with our actions.

That is not to say that we have been overly influenced by the Protestant liberal mind-set, although most American Catholics today have, to some extent, been culturally influenced by it and the values it promotes. This statement, however, has struck a chord within us about our own rendering of and accountability to the Catholic faith. It reminds us of how the various aspects of that faith are so deeply intertwined. Everything in the faith is connected, to put it plainly, including all doctrinal truths.

A subtle change in emphasis in one particular teaching will bring about a corresponding shift in many others. To cite just one example, a shift in our understanding of Jesus (e.g., emphasizing his humanity over his divinity) will have major ramifications for the way we understand the church and our role in it. That, in turn, affects the way we understand the church's relationship to the world and, by way of extension, the world's relation to the kingdom. The point being made here is that a shift in just one aspect of our theological outlook will have a ripple effect on the whole.

A Basic Shift

It has now become commonplace to speak of a fundamental change that took place in Catholic thought following the Second Vatican Council. The process of *aggiornamento* initiated by Pope John XXIII when calling the Council spread through the church like wildfire. After centuries of maintaining a defensive, fortress mentality toward the world, the church encouraged Catholics to open up to the world and engage it in dialogue. To use another nomenclature coined by Niebuhr, the church came out of a "Christ against culture" understanding of its role in the world to a stance that looked to "Christ as the transformer of culture."[4]

This shift in attitude toward the world influenced the church's own self-understanding, especially with regard to its past. In their attempt to keep pace with the changes going on in the world and, perforce, now in the church, many of the Catholic faithful — clergy, religious, and laity alike — looked down upon or simply did away with many beliefs and practices that, after centuries of inclusion, had become an important part of their self-identity (e.g., weekly confession, Friday abstinence, numerous private devotions). In the haste and enthusiasm of the moment, some got carried away and disregarded or at least assigned lesser significance to aspects of the faith that really should have remained in the mainstream of Catholic spirituality.

With regard to the church's teaching on the final judgment, the popular post–Vatican II shift from a high Christology (emphasizing Christ's divinity) to a low Christology (emphasizing his humanity) brought about a similar shift in emphasis regarding Christ's action in the world. Rather than focusing on Christ's dominion and Lordship over heaven and earth, the shift to a low Christology emphasized Jesus' solidarity with and love for humanity. Jesus became more of a friend and brother than a lawgiver and judge, someone to whom we could turn in time of need rather than someone to hide from for fear of the punishment of our sins.

Such a shift in emphasis was healthy and good, but only within certain limits. To call Jesus our friend and brother is certainly a welcome change from the exaggerated adulation accorded to him during the years immediately preceding the Council. But along with this change also came an imaginal misconstruing of Jesus' person and mission.

Is not calling Jesus our friend and brother nothing but another confining stereotype? Can we honestly say that it fully captures the fullness of his life and message? Decades later the delicate balance between the divine and human elements in Christ still remains out of sync in the popular Catholic imagination, so much so that one has to wonder if the change in attitude toward Christ that came about in the aftermath of Vatican II succeeded only in replacing one false image of God with another.

False God to False God

Over forty years ago, J. B. Phillips, an Anglican priest best known for his translation of the New Testament into Modern English, wrote a book entitled, *Your God Is Too Small*. In it, he attempts: "... first to expose the inadequate conceptions of God which still linger unconsciously in many minds and which prevent our catching a glimpse of the true God; and secondly to suggest ways in which we can find the real God for ourselves."[5]

Phillips states that there are many false images of God that people possess and find very hard to shake. God can be thought of as a resident policeman, a demanding parent, a grand old man, a meek and mild companion, the embodiment of perfection, a heavenly lover, a managing director, a pale Galilean, a projected image, and assorted combinations of these and other stereotypes.[6] Phillips concludes that, in order to have an adequate understanding of the divine, we must recognize that God, while infinitely beyond the powers of human comprehension, planned a concrete focusing of himself in the person of Jesus Christ.[7] Jesus alone reveals the mystery of God to us. To find God in our lives we must encounter this person and allow him to show us the true way of living. What does this mean concretely?

Our faith tells us that Jesus Christ is fully human *and* fully divine. If this is so, then we should relate to him as such and do all we can to insure that he exists that way in our active imagination. To emphasize Christ's divinity at the expense of his humanity, or vice versa, is merely to substitute one false image of God for another.

While the church has been careful to maintain this delicate balance in its doctrinal expressions, it has not always been successful doing so in the popular imagination. Prior to the Second Vatican Council, Catholic piety and devotion tended to accentuate the divinity of Christ over his humanity. In the decades following the Council, the reverse emphasis took precedence. At the dawn of the new millennium, we have been called to strike down our false images of Christ so that we can have a more adequate understanding of God's presence in our lives. We can do so, however, only by giving both Christ's divinity *and* his humanity a proper place in our hearts.

Contemplating the Face of Christ

In *Novo Millennio Ineuente,* his apostolic letter on the church in the Third Millennium, the late Pope John Paul II emphasized the importance of prayer for the future of the church, especially contemplative prayer. He bid Christians the world over to contemplate the face of Christ so that the Spirit of Christ might touch and inspire them to follow the way of love.[8]

When we contemplate that face, the false images we have of God gradually break up and lose their hold over us. Jesus dispels our stereotypes and reveals to us the power of the divine in the fullness of his humanity. This happens by means of a mutual, reciprocal gaze, similar to the way a bridegroom fixes his eyes on his beloved and receives a silent, affectionate response.

It begins when we open our hearts to him in prayer and become still in his presence. We look into his eyes and allow him to look into ours. We peer into his soul, and he peers into ours. We get to know him, and he gets to know us. In the midst of this stillness, we experience Jesus in the depths of our hearts. We gaze upon his humanity and touch the mystery of his divinity. He, in turn, gazes upon our humanity and sees there the person each of us is destined to become.

In the Gospel of John, Jesus refers to himself as the light of the world (see Jn 9:5). He dispels the darkness from our hearts and enables us to see ourselves for who we really are. The church's teaching on the last judgment must be seen through the lens of this important scriptural saying. Christ brings to light all that is secret, all the hidden betrayals, all the subtle compromises, and all the self-deceptions that have crept into our lives over the years.

When we contemplate the face of Christ, the light of his truth penetrates every fiber of our being and enables us to peer into the deepest recesses of our hearts. We are able to see things as they really are. Judgment, in this sense, is nothing more than bringing to light our deepest aspirations. We spend our whole lives cultivating these hopes. Once revealed, we are free to respond as we wish. We chose to walk either toward or away from Christ. The grace to do so is his; the choice is entirely our own.

True Judgment, False Judgment

With regard to the final judgment, the Catholic imagination in recent decades has been subjected to the influence of opposing extremes. For centuries prior to the Second Vatican Council, an emphasis on the divinity and Lordship of Christ brought the threat of judgment to the fore of Catholic spirituality. The following description from a noted author is typical of mainstream Catholic teaching of the time: "The coming of the Judge will be preceded by fire. Fire will descend from heaven, and shall burn the earth and all things upon the earth. Thus palaces, churches, villas, cities, kingdoms, all must be reduced to one heap of ashes. This house, defiled by sin, must be purified by fire."[9] When combined with false images of God that presented him as an exacting taskmaster who kept a full account of our sins and who would demand a complete reckoning at the end of time, this emphasis made us deeply afraid of both God (for fear of what he might do to us) and of living life (for fear of making a mistake).

After Vatican II, this false notion of final judgment was gradually replaced by an equally false and misconceived perception. God, the vengeful judge, was replaced by a God who closes his eyes or simply looks the other way. Somehow during the course of the post–Vatican II era, many of the Catholic faithful (clergy, religious, and laity) have managed to put the church's teaching on the final judgment so far back on the back burner of Catholic spirituality that it now has little, if any, vital and lasting impact on their lives.

With no concrete assessment of human action on the horizon of human destiny, the ethical quality of our actions diminishes and can easily veer in the direction of moral relativism. The question facing us today is how we can strike both false images from the popular consciousness of Catholic spirituality and put a more balanced understanding of final judgment in its place.

As noted in this book's introduction, C. S. Lewis's creative depiction of Deep Heaven may well be the place to begin. It captures our imagination, strikes down these false images, and reminds us of an important Christian belief regarding the nature of human happiness: "There are only two kinds of people in the end: those who say to God, 'Thy will be done,' and those to whom God says, in the end, '*Thy* will be done.' All that are in Hell, choose it. Without that self-choice there would be no Hell."[10]

Those who have made their way to Deep Heaven, by way of contrast, resonate strongly with the words of the psalmist, "I delight to do your will, O my God; your law is within my heart" (Ps 40:8). Even though their journey has taken them beyond the pale of death, their hearts still resonate with Ronald Rolheiser's description of delight: "You feel your own life — your heart, your mind, your body, your sexuality, the people and things you are connected to — and you spontaneously fill with the exclamation: 'God, it feels great to be alive!' "[11] "Man's primordial impulse," Pope Benedict XVI reminds us, "is his desire for happiness and an entirely fulfilled life."[12]

We become happy and entirely fulfilled when we freely receive and reciprocate love that comes from God. The joy of Deep Heaven, its wonder, its depth, its mystery, lies hidden in this mutual indwelling of God and humanity.

Conclusion

The next time we recite the Nicene Creed at Sunday Mass and come to the words about Christ coming again in glory to judge the living and the dead, perhaps we should pause and ask ourselves how firmly we hold that belief and what it really means to us. Beatitude and happiness go hand in hand. For too long, the Catholic imagination has lost touch with the powerful truth about humanity's final destiny. We have become lazy practitioners of the faith, allowing the doctrinal truths of our religion to pass readily from our lips before resounding deep in our hearts. Rather than simply settling for the way things are or, perhaps even worse, reverting to the false understanding of final judgment in vogue in an earlier period in time, we need to find ways of sparking our imagination today so that the truths of the faith, mysterious and difficult to comprehend as they may be, can penetrate our longing hearts and minds and guide us boldly and assuredly during our journey to Deep Heaven.

Reflection Questions

1. Do you believe that Jesus will come again in glory? That there will be a last judgment of the living and dead? That his kingdom will be without end? If so, why do you believe these things? If not, why not?

Which of these beliefs do you find the most difficult to accept?

2. Do you have any inadequate or false conceptions of God that linger in the back of your mind and influence your actions? If so, can you describe them? How can you be free of them? In what way have these false images shaped your understanding of the church's teaching on the last judgment?

3. What does it mean to contemplate the face of Christ? How does one allow the light of his truth to penetrate every fiber of one's being so that one can see things as they really are? In what ways do you bring to the surface and cultivate your deepest hopes?

4. Do you agree that the doctrine of the last judgment has lost its hold over the Catholic imagination? If so, do you view this change in a positive or a negative light? What, to your mind, has captured the Catholic imagination today? What are the positive and negative aspects of this change in outlook?

5. Do you believe in Deep Heaven? If so, what is it like? If not, what do you believe happens at the end of the world as we know it? In what ways does God allow us to choose our own destiny?

Praying for Deep Heaven

I long for you, Lord, and I long for Deep Heaven.

When I ponder your return in glory to bring an end to all things and to render your final judgment over the living and the dead, I see you not as a harsh, exacting judge, but as a loving brother who has come once more, this time at the end of time and space as we know it, to preach your message of love and forgiveness to a stubborn and forgetful people.

I believe you will come again in glory, Lord, to judge the living and the dead, but I believe that this judgment will ultimately be nothing more than what we have already chosen for ourselves.

You will force no one to enter Deep Heaven against their will.

We ourselves must chose to enter there, and to do so we must let go of our petty concerns and self-interest and trust in you.

Thank you, Lord, for seeking us out this one final time.

Help us, Lord, to see the light of your truth and to open our hearts to you in love and friendship.

Help me, Lord, help me.

Help me to keep my final end always before my eyes.

Help me to live my life with this end always in view.

Help me to reach out to others in a way that will help them to focus on the end for which they were made.

Help me, Lord, to make my longing for Deep Heaven visible so that others might get a glimpse of what is yet to come.

Epilogue

Further Up and Further In

Then, still looking at his face, I saw there something that sent a quiver through my whole body. I stood at that moment with my back to the East and the mountains, and he, facing me, looked toward them. His face was flushed with a new light. A fern, thirty yards behind him, turned golden. The eastern side of every tree-trunk grew bright. Shadows deepened. All the time there had been bird noises, trillings, chatterings, and the like; but now suddenly the full chorus was poured from every branch; cocks were crowing, there was music of hounds, and horns; above all this ten thousand tongues of men and woodland angels and the wood itself sang. "It comes! It comes!" they sang. "Sleepers awake! It comes, it comes, it comes."
— C. S. Lewis, *The Great Divorce*

IN THIS BOOK we have looked at six important beliefs about Jesus that ought to have a strong impact on us:

> *his incarnate birth*
> *his passion and death*
> *his descent into hell*

> *his resurrection from the dead*
> *his ascension into heaven*
> *his return in glory at the end of time.*

Because of our friendship with Christ, these beliefs should not be for us mere abstract doctrines with little or no relevance for our daily lives, but vital, living truths that shape the way we live and profess our faith. They also remind us of the kind of people we are called to become as we make our way to our true and final home in Deep Heaven.

C. S. Lewis once called joy "the serious business of Heaven."[1] By this he meant that human beings were meant for God and would not experience the fullness of life until they saw him face to face. This sentiment reflects very well the famous words of St. Augustine: "You so excite him that to praise You is his joy. You have made us for Yourself, O Lord, and our hearts are restless until they rest in You."[2]

Deep Heaven, for Lewis, has to do with the experience of longing to enter ever more deeply into the mystery of God. One of his most imaginative and memorable renderings of Deep Heaven comes in *The Last Battle,* the final volume of his children's fantasy, *The Chronicles of Narnia,* when he describes how evil infects the land of Narnia and how Aslan, the Lion King, a figure of Christ throughout the tales, leads his people to a glorious new world. This new Narnia resembles the old, but conveys a sense of being deeper, richer, indeed, more real:

> It is as hard to explain how this sunlit land was different from the old Narnia, as it would be to tell you how the fruits of that country taste. Perhaps you will

get some idea of it, if you think like this. You may have been in a room in which there was a window that looked out on a lovely bay of the sea or a green valley that wound away among mountains. And in the wall of that room opposite to the window there may have been a looking glass. And as you turned away from the window you suddenly caught sight of the sea or that valley, all over again, in the looking glass. And the sea in the mirror, or the valley in the mirror, were in one sense just the same as the real ones: yet at the same time they were somehow different — deeper, more wonderful, more like places in a story: in a story you have never heard but very much want to know. The difference between the old Narnia and the new Narnia was like that. The new one was a deeper country: every rock and flower and blade of grass looked as if it meant more. I can't describe it any better than that: if you ever get there, you will know what I mean.

It was the Unicorn who summed up what everyone was feeling. He stamped his right fore-hoof on the ground and neighed and then cried:

"I have come home at last! This is my real country! I belong here. This is the land I have been looking for all my life, though I never knew it until now. The reason why we loved the old Narnia is that it sometimes looked a little like this. Bree-hee-hee! Come further up, come further in!"[3]

Jesus once said: "Truly I tell you, whoever does not receive the kingdom of God as a little child will never enter it" (Mk 10:15).

We need the eyes of a child to sense both the nearness of the kingdom and the loving relationship with God that we have been called to share. May this simple saying of Jesus and this brief scene from a work of a master storyteller work together to spark our imagination and lead us to believe more firmly in the reality of Deep Heaven and the joy of another world that far exceeds our deepest dreams and wildest expectations.

Notes

Introduction

1. C. S. Lewis, *The Great Divorce* (New York: Macmillan, 1946), 66–67.

2. Ibid.

3. C. S. Lewis, *Surprised by Joy: The Shape of My Early Life* (New York: Harcourt, Brace & World, 1955), 17–18. Throughout this book, I use the terms "happiness" and "joy" interchangeably. The distinction between them made by C. S. Lewis (*Surprised by Joy*, 17–18) refers to the state of "imperfect earthly beatitude" and is not applicable to their use in language for describing the perfect beatitude of Deep Heaven. In this beatific state, the categories of "joy," "happiness," and even "pleasure," merge into one.

4. Ronald Rolheiser, *The Holy Longing: The Search for a Christian Spirituality* (New York: Doubleday, 1999), 26.

5. Thomas Merton, *Seeds of Contemplation* (London: Catholic Book Club, 1950), 32.

6. C. S. Lewis, *The Problem of Pain* (New York: Macmillan, 1962; fourteenth printing, 1973), 147–48.

7. Alphonsus de Liguori, *The Way to Converse Always and Familiarly with God* in *The Complete Works of Saint Alphonsus de Liguori*, vol. 2, ed. Eugene Grimm, *The Way of Salvation and Perfection* (Brooklyn: Redemptorist Fathers, 1926), 395.

8. Attributed to Socrates (469–399 BCE).

9. Augustine of Hippo, *Confessions*, bk. 7, chap. 21. Cited in Lewis, *Surprised by Joy*, 230.

Chapter One

1. C. S. Lewis, "Myth Became Fact," in *God in the Dock: Essays on Theology and Ethics,* ed. Walter Hooper (Grand Rapids, MI: Wm. B. Eerdmans, 1970), 66.

2. C. S. Lewis, *Surprised by Joy: The Shape of My Early Life* (New York: Harcourt, Brace & World, 1955), 236.

3. From "The Apostles' Creed" in *The Roman Missal: The Sacramentary* (New York: Catholic Book Publishing Co., 1985), 369.

4. C. S. Lewis, "The Grand Miracle," in *God in the Dock,* 80–88.

5. Athanasius of Alexandria, *De incarnatione,* 54.3, in *Sources chrétiennes,* 199.458–59 (PG 25.191–92).

6. Irenaeus of Lyons, *Against Heresies,* 4.20.5–7, in *Sources chrétiennes,* 100.640–42, 644–48.

7. Hans Urs von Balthasar, *A Theological Anthropology* (New York: Sheed and Ward, 1967), 249.

8. For Eckhardt's "Sermon on the Eternal Birth," see *Late Medieval Mysticism,* The Library of Christian Classics, ed. Ray C. Petry (Philadelphia: Westminster Press, 1957), 177–92.

9. See the introduction above, n. 7.

Chapter Two

1. C. S. Lewis, *Mere Christianity* (New York: Macmillan, 1943; seventeenth printing, 1973), 58.

2. Ibid.

3. From "The Apostles' Creed" in *The Roman Missal,* 369.

4. Lewis, *Mere Christianity,* 57.

5. Horace Bushnell, *The Vicarious Sacrifice* (1866). Cited in Kenneth Leech, *Experiencing God: Theology as Spirituality* (San Francisco: Harper and Row, 1985; paperback ed., 1989), 301.

6. C. S. Lewis, *The Four Loves* (San Diego: Harcourt, Brace Jovanovich, 1960), 53–192.

7. See *Summa theologiae,* II-II, q. 23, a. 1, resp.

8. Lewis, *Mere Christianity,* 58.

Chapter Three

1. C. S. Lewis, *The Problem of Pain* (New York: Macmillan, 1962; fourteenth printing, 1973), 125–26.

2. Ibid., 127.

3. The *Catechism of the Catholic Church* (nos. 631–37) uses the phrase "descended into hell"; the English translation of the Apostles' Creed sometimes used at Mass reads, "descended to the dead."

4. C. S. Lewis, *The Great Divorce* (New York: Macmillan, 1946), 18–19.

5. Ronald Rolheiser, *The Restless Heart: Finding Our Spiritual Home in Times of Loneliness* (New York: Doubleday, 2004), 43.

6. For more on iconography and Jesus' descent into hell, see M. Helen Weier, *Festal Icons of the Lord* (Collegeville, MN: Liturgical Press, 1977), 41–44.

7. Lewis, *The Problem of Pain*, 128.

8. Cited in C. S. Lewis, *Surprised by Joy: The Shape of My Early Life* (New York: Harcourt, Brace & World, 1955), 212.

9. Lewis, *The Problem of Pain*, 123.

10. Ibid., 125–26.

11. C. S. Lewis, *The Abolition of Man* (New York: Macmillan, 1947; tenth printing, 1973), 83–84.

12. Lewis, *The Problem of Pain*, 127.

13. Ibid.

Chapter Four

1. C. S. Lewis, *Miracles* (New York: Macmillan, 1947; 10th printing, 1971), 153.

2. Ibid., 148.

3. Ibid., 150.

4. Ibid.

5. Ibid., 116.

6. Ibid., 157.

7. Ibid., 160–61.

8. C. S. Lewis, *The Problem of Pain* (New York: Macmillan, 1962; fourteenth printing, 1973), 147.

Chapter Five

1. C. S. Lewis, *Miracles* (New York: Macmillan, 1947; 10th printing, 1971), 153.

2. Ibid., 154.

3. Ibid., 152.

4. Ibid., 162.

5. Ibid., 163.

6. Fabio Giardini, *Pray without Ceasing: Toward a Systematic Psychotheology of Christian Prayerlife* (Leominster, Hertfordshire: Gracewing, and Rome: Millennium, 1998), 143.

7. Ibid., 141–93.

8. Ibid. 195–278.

9. Ibid., 300.

10. Ibid., 375, 391–92.

11. C. S. Lewis, *Reflections on the Psalms* (New York: Harcourt, Brace & World, 1958), 133.

12. Ibid., 143–44. For the dynamic integration of all of these forms of prayer, see Giardini, *Pray without Ceasing*, 279–301.

13. Lewis, *Reflections on the Psalms*, 134.

14. See *Catechism of the Catholic Church*, no. 2634.

15. C. S. Lewis, *Letters to Malcolm: Chiefly on Prayer* (New York: Harcourt, Brace, Jovanovich, 1964), 77.

16. Ibid., 91.

17. Ibid., 21.

18. Giardini, *Pray without Ceasing*, 279–301.

19. Lewis, *Letters to Malcolm*, 21.

20. Lewis, *Miracles*, 154.

Chapter Six

1. See *Catechism of the Catholic Church*, nos. 668–82.

2. *The Roman Missal, The Sacramentary,* 370.

3. H. Richard Niebuhr, *The Kingdom of God in America* (New York: Harper & Brothers, 1937), 193.

4. H. Richard Niebuhr, *Christ and Culture* (New York: Harper and Row, 1951; reprint, Harper Torchbooks, 1956), esp. 45–82, 190–229.

5. J. B. Phillips, *Your God Is Too Small* (New York: Macmillan, 1961; 6th printing, 1967), 8–9.

6. See Ibid., 15–59.

7. Ibid., 120–24.

8. John Paul II, *Novo Millennio Ineuente* (January 6, 2001), nos. 16–28. The English translation is available on the Internet at *www.vatican.va.*

9. Alphonsus de Liguori, *Preparation for Death* in *The Complete Works of St. Alphonsus de Liguori,* vol. 1, ed. Eugene Grimm (New York: Benziger Brothers, 1886; reprint ed., Brooklyn: Redemptorist Fathers, 1926), 252.

10. C. S. Lewis, *The Great Divorce* (New York: Macmillan, 1946), 72.

11. Ronald Rolheiser, *The Holy Longing: The Search for a Christian Spirituality* (New York: Doubleday, 1999), 26.

12. Pope Benedict XVI, "Address to the Pontifical Biblical Commission," April 27, 2006; cited in "God Guarantees Happiness, Affirms Pope," ZENIT, Archive Date: 2006-04-27 (see *www.zenit.org/english*).

Epilogue

1. C. S. Lewis, *Letters to Malcolm: Chiefly on Prayer* (New York: Harcourt Brace, Jovanovich, 1964), 93.

2. Augustine of Hippo, *Confessions,* bk. 1, chap. 1. Adapted from *The Confessions of St. Augustine,* trans. F. J. Sheed (New York: Sheed and Ward, 1943), 3.

3. C. S. Lewis, *The Last Battle* in *The Chronicles of Narnia,* vol. 7 (New York: Collier Books, 1956; 10th printing, 1974), 170–71.

green press
INITIATIVE

Paulist Press is committed to preserving ancient forests and natural resources. We elected to print this title on 30% post consumer recycled paper, processed chlorine free. As a result, for this printing, we have saved:

> 4 Trees (40' tall and 6-8" diameter)
> 1,404 Gallons of Wastewater
> 3 million BTU's of Total Energy
> 180 Pounds of Solid Waste
> 338 Pounds of Greenhouse Gases

Paulist Press made this paper choice because our printer, Thomson-Shore, Inc., is a member of Green Press Initiative, a nonprofit program dedicated to supporting authors, publishers, and suppliers in their efforts to reduce their use of fiber obtained from endangered forests.

For more information, visit www.greenpressinitiative.org

Environmental impact estimates were made using the Environmental Defense Paper Calculator. For more information visit: www.papercalculator.org.